SPORTING INCIDENTS

IN THE

LIFE OF ANOTHER TOM SMITH,

MASTER OF FOXHOUNDS;
AUTHOR OF "THE DIARY OF A HUNTSMAN," ETC.

With Illustrations.

LONDON:

CHAPMAN AND HALL, 193 PICCADILLY.

1867.

ADVERTISEMENT.

THE following pages contain some notices of
the life of Thomas Smith, Ex-Master of Fox-
hounds, and the keenest sportsman that I at
least have ever known. He was not, it is true,
born with a silver spoon in his mouth, like
Tom Smith of Tedworth, with whom he ran
a long course of honourable rivalry; but he
was, as I may say, "born in the saddle,"
which is more to the purpose for a true sportsman.

During his long career, Mr. Smith has been
twice Master of the Hambledon Hounds; he
has also been Master of the Craven and of the
Pytchley; he has hunted with most of the
best packs in the kingdom; and he has had a
good deal of sport in Scotland, where he made
havoc among the salmon and the grouse, as

well as looking sharply after the four-footed
feræ naturæ. In 1852 he retired from his last
Mastership with a handsome testimonial. But
the public had not yet done with him. He
was called on in 1858 to serve the office of
High Sheriff for Hampshire, the duties of
which post he discharged with zeal and ability.
He now lives, and long may he live, "a prosperous gentleman," in the centre of the Hambledon Hunt; and so well has he carried his
years, that he is still an effective member of
the First Hants Light Horse (better known as
the Droxford Foxhunters' Corps), a force that
he was instrumental in first suggesting.

During his sporting career, Mr. Smith has
performed feats and met with adventures that
probably no other man has equalled. And this
is not my opinion alone. Mr. Nichol, who
kept the New Forest hounds, usually spoke of
him as "the heaven-born huntsman;" and Mr.
Codrington, who hunted the same pack, said,
"Were I a fox, I would rather have a pack of
hounds behind me than Tom Smith with a
stick in his hand." Several of Mr. Smith's

friends have therefore thought it advisable that some of these matters should be put in print, whilst the eye-witnesses of many of them are still alive, so that there may be no cavilling about them at a future day. Indeed this is the consideration, and the only consideration, that has induced our old friend to consent to their being brought forward during his lifetime. The particulars are all taken from his own lips, and I have never found him to vary even in the most minute manner. Should any one express his surprise at any of them, I can only reply, in Mr. Smith's own words, " If any one states the exact truth at first, he can repeat it a thousand times without faltering;" which is a piece of good advice that young sportsmen would do well always to bear in mind.

In conclusion, I hope that this volume will have interest for more than one class of readers. It shows that Mr. Smith is a staunch fox-hunter, and a good deal more beside. Many useful inventions have been the fruit of his fertile brain, ranging from the improvement of pastures and the preservation of fruit, to the "Iron-Duke" bit and a locomotive battery; and he has also found time to offer suggestions as to recruiting, military colonies in India, the improvement of the metropolis, &c., to the proper authorities, which H.R.H. the Duke of Cambridge, Lord Palmerston, and others have thought well worth consideration.

Although the following reminiscences are tolerably numerous, yet I believe that a sufficient number of useful hints and interesting facts can be added, if Mr. Smith can be prevailed on to take the trouble of relating them, to fill another volume or two.

A FRIEND.

CONTENTS.

————✦✦✦————

CHAPTER I.

PAGE

School-boy days—Early activity and habits of observation — An ugly wound — An election anecdote —
Volunteering—First scarlet coat   1

CHAPTER II.

Farming — Vice-President of the Winchester Agricultural Show — Fox-hunting — Cricket—Devon Stag-
hounds—Marriage—Residence at Hill House, Hambledon — Visit to Scotland — Lord Fife's practical
jokes—Mr. Owen, of New Lanark—An unpleasant
mistake—Adventure in a coal-mine—"Out of debt,
out of danger" 19

CHAPTER III.

Sport in the New Forest—Sir Bellingham Graham—The
horse General—Mr. Smith becomes Master of the
Hambledon hounds —Unpromising beginning—Extraordinary run into Sussex—Mr. Smith's picture of
the H. H., with sixty-five likenesses—Visit to the
Quorn—An unexpected honour   39

CHAPTER IV.

PAGE

The Hambledon pack increased—A perilous adventure
—Anecdote of Lord Palmerston—Accidents—Hard
riding—Removal to Swanmere—Death of Mrs. Smith
—Society at Exton—Sir Joseph Yorke and others—
Visit to London—Resigns the Hambledon hounds   .   64

CHAPTER V.

Becomes Master of the Craven Hunt—A daring leap—
The horse General—Repartee of Mr. Warde—Anecdote of· H.R.H. the Duke of Gloucester—Troubles
with young hounds—" A haunch of fox"—The Grey
Withers—The Swing riots—Gives up the Craven   .   86

CHAPTER VI.

Second marriage—A theory on Stonehenge—Mr. Beckford's Letter on the Rights of Fox·hunters—Publishes " The Diary of a Huntsman"—A run with the
Royal stag-hounds—Death of Vampire—Plan for
kennels and stabling   104

CHAPTER VII.

Declines the offer of various Hunts—Visit to Scotland—
Residence in Dorsetshire—" Tremulous to her new
Master"   121

CHAPTER VIII.

Becomes Master of the Pytchley Hunt—Management of
the hounds—Difficulties—Lord Spencer—Kind conduct of the Duke of Buccleuch—Extraordinary runs

PAGE

—Resigns the Pytchley—Hints on buying horses—
An unpleasant adventure 131

CHAPTER IX.

Visits to Scotland, Yorkshire, &c.—Sir Tatton Sykes'
establishment at Edlesthorpe—Anecdote of Sir Tatton—Castle Howard: runs with various packs—
Anecdote of Lady Morgan—Visit to the Continent—
Kindness of Mr. N. M. Rothschild and his family . 157

CHAPTER X.

Returns to England, and resumes the Mastership of the
Hambledon hounds—Purchases the Fir Hill estate,
Droxford—His "Good-bye Day" 174

CHAPTER XI.

Publishes "The Life of a Fox, written by himself"—
Visits the Duke of Beaufort at Badminton, and
Lord Fitzhardinge—The bull-dogs and the bear . 197

CHAPTER XII.

Life at Fir Hill—Serves the office of High Sheriff of
Hants—Various suggestions and improvements . 207

Directions for placing the Plates.

———✦❋✦———

Portrait of Mr. Smith—*to face Title-page*   PAGE

Taking a Sparrow's Nest   4

Over Lyndhurst New Park Paling   41

Taking the Stag   43

Awful Leap with the Quorne Hounds   56

Swiming across a River   66

Leap over Elcot Park Wall   89

Building up of Stonehenge   105

Raising of the Stones   106

Two old Stags fastened together by their Antlers .   .   151

Plan of Cottages with three Bedrooms   208

Design for a Locomotive Battery   212

Plan for the Thames Embankment   215

MEMOIR OF TOM SMITH.

CHAPTER I.

School-boy days—Early activity and habits of observation—
An ugly wound—An election anecdote—Volunteering—
First scarlet coat.

TOM SMITH, the son of Mr. Thomas and Martha
Smith, of Shalden Lodge, near Alton, in the
county of Hants, was born there August 5th,
1790. He was the eldest of nine sons, who
all had to make their own way in the world;
and, on the recommendation of Dr. Reynolds,
then Dean of Winchester, he was sent to Eton,
being intended for the Church. He, however,
remained but a short time at that famous seat
of learning; for he showed such a decided
liking for active habits and field sports, that

his father was induced to remove him, sending in his place his next brother, Samuel, now Vicar of Weedon Lois, in Northamptonshire. Two other brothers also became clergymen; two others entered the army; one became a sailor; another a barrister; and the ninth died young, as did also one of his sisters; the eldest daughter married Colonel Johnston; and the second married Mr. James Ward, a county magistrate.

Tom's next school was at Holybourne, not very far from home, and where he had plenty of opportunities for "sport" in a small way, which he eagerly engaged in, being not at all daunted by an awkward adventure that befell him in one of his holidays. In common with most country-bred boys, bird-nesting had great charms for him, and in pursuing this diversion he narrowly escaped with his life on one occasion. He had noticed a sparrow's nest in the roof of his father's cart-house, and this he determined to get. He induced one of

the men to place a long ladder for him, which
he ascended; but he then found the nest almost beyond his reach. Determined not to be
foiled, he stretched out at full length over a
lath, and had just grasped the prize, when
away went the ladder from under him, and he
was left hanging to the lath by one hand, as
he is represented in the accompanying sketch,
which he made at the request of a friend many
years after. A boy of only ordinary nerve
would have dropped to the ground in a minute
or two, and been either killed on the spot, or
crippled for life, for the height was at least
forty feet; but Tom Smith, though only twelve
years old, had a good share of the extraordinary nerve that he has since had the opportunity of showing in divers "moving *accidents*
by flood and field," and was equal to the
emergency. He was alone, and though he
screamed for help, he had little hope of receiving it; so he at once set about helping
himself. He thrust his disengaged hand be-

tween the thatch and the rafter, about a foot
below his first hold, then abandoned that and
made a clutch lower down, and "rung the
changes" in this way several times, although
of course the shock each time was terrific, and
seemed enough to dislocate the arm; but he
persevered, and at length thus reached a beam,
along which he crawled until he came over
a wagon, into which he dropped, without
broken bones, but fearfully exhausted, and
with hands quite benumbed.

Mr. Thomas Smith was himself a great fox-
hunter and a bold rider, and he allowed his
son, when at home for the Christmas holidays,
to worry the hares on his land, by "hunting"
them with every cur that he could get. In
this sport Tom took great delight, and he
looked on himself as already a "Master of
Hounds," although his "pack" was rather a
motley one. In this sport he was joined by
other boys in the parish, and more than one
"hard rider" in after days has been heard to

H. DELL.

LONDON: CHAPMAN & HALL, 193, PICCADILLY 1866.

DAY & SON LIMITED. LITH

T. SMITH WHEN A BOY 12 YEARS OLD TAKING A SPARROWS NEST
KICKED THE LADDER AWAY AS DESCRIBED AND WAS LEFT 28 FEET FROM THE GROUND.

own Tom Smith as his instructor. This was particularly the case with Douglas Standen, afterwards Colonel Standen, a particularly bold rider, and a man totally indifferent to falls. He always ascribed both these qualifications for a keen sportsman to the instructions of his first riding-master, Tom Smith, who taught him to sit loose on his pony and lean back when riding over or through a fence. But however great a man's nerve may be in early life, it is liable to be destroyed by a sudden shock. This happened with Colonel Cummins, one of the boldest riders in the H.H. country, residing at that time at Burkham, three miles from Shaldon, and who often encouraged the young fox-hunter by giving him a gingerbread nut or sandwich. The Colonel, however, left Burkham and went abroad. A few years after this he returned, and went in a low pony-chair to make inquiries as to Mr. Smith's family, when his young friend expressed his great delight at the hope of seeing him ride

again in his usual bold and straightforward
manner; and as the Colonel was not yet provided with a horse, he most urgently offered
to lend him his own, when he was surprised by the Colonel holding up both hands
as if shocked at the thought, exclaiming at
the same time, "Ride your hunter! I would not
get on the back of your horse, or any horse in
the world, on any account whatever; I have
entirely lost my nerve ever since my adventure in Italy." This he related as follows:
"When travelling in Italy, and sleeping at an
inn not famed for its good character, I had
fastened my bedroom door by an additional
matter of my own, that is, with a stout walk-
ing-stick, having a spike at each end,—one
stuck into the floor, and the other into the
door. After lying quiet, as if asleep, for some
time, in the middle of the night I heard a
noise opposite the foot of the bed, and saw
that part of a panel was gently moving; next,
with my eyes nearly closed, I saw a man come

up to my bedside with a dark lantern in his
hand, which he opened, and placed the light
close to my face, in order to see whether I was
awake or asleep. I succeeded in deceiving
him, and he quietly took my watch, purse, and
pocket-book from under my pillow; and, after
looking over other things in the room, he was
retiring, hoping to unfasten the door: when
doing this, I sprang suddenly out of bed and
on to the man's back, with my arms and hands
so firmly fast round him that, although he
knocked my head against the posts and wall,
and then ran down stairs with me on his back,
and carried me out into the street—by which
time my calls for help were heard, and the
rascal was secured—it required the strength
of three men to unlock my arms from the
man's neck. This, then, is the cause of my
having entirely lost my nerve; but I saved
my money and my watch, &c., and my life."

But with all their efforts, the young sportsmen, we believe, never killed a hare; and

Tom, who ever liked variety, never missed
an opportunity of sport of any other kind.   So
he was ever ready to act as marker to the parties of shooters that his father often enter-
tained; and they were the gainers from the
extraordinary aptitude that he showed for
marking a covey.   But he was very near doing
this once too often.   It happened, when he
was on a visit at Marlow, that he was out
with his uncle and another gentleman; and,
when passing by the side of a young hedge-
row, the pointer stood at a rabbit.   Tom was
told to go on the other side and throw a stone
to drive the rabbit towards the shooters.   He
was about to do so, when the rabbit started,
both gentlemen fired, and down went their
young marker, apparently killed.   Each ac-
cusing the other as the author of the mischief,
they rushed towards him, and found a hole
the size of a crown-piece in his hat.   This
redoubled their fears; but they found he was
only stunned, and, placing him on the shooting

pony, they carried him to the doctor. A full
charge of shot was taken out of his head, and
afterwards shown to him in a wine-glass; but
one shot that had lodged in his right hand
(which had been in a line with the hole in the
hat) was not noticed at the time, and it still
remains there.

At one of the Hampshire elections, when
Sir H. Mildmay and Mr. Chute were candi-
dates, Mr. Smith was an active canvasser on
their behalf, and Tom had an opportunity of
seeing of what stuff the "independent elector"
was then made. Of course, such things are
out of date now. An Alton butcher named
Boswell had promised his vote, and Mr. Smith
went, accompanied by Tom, in a carriage to
convey him to the poll; but they found
another carriage at the butcher's door, and
learnt, without surprise, that he had promised
the other party also. Each canvasser, it appeared, had "staked money on his head," and
an edifying dialogue ensued. At last it was

agreed that they should toss up for the butcher. Mr. Smith won, and carried him off; but he was obliged to keep a very sharp eye on his man until he had voted. Mr. George Rose, the "old George Rose" whom Cobbett used to abuse so much, was on a visit to Mr. Smith soon after; he pronounced this as pretty a piece of electioneering as ever he had known, and he had the credit of understanding such matters.

Among the visitors to Mr. Smith was, on one occasion, the Duc de Bourbon (the father of the unfortunate Duc d'Enghien), who came for a little sport, accompanied by a servant carrying two double-barrelled guns: he was then a guest of Lord Elcho, at South Warnborough, not far from Shaldon. Though very young at the time, Tom well remembers the stately royal emigrant, and the tears that he shed at seeing, in the dining-room at Shaldon, a picture representing the capture of the Bastille.

Beside hunting in his own small way, Tom was allowed by his father now and then to join the Hampshire hounds, at that time under the management of Mr. Joseph Russell, who kept them at Grewell, a few miles only from Shaldon. Will Harrison, the old huntsman, used good-naturedly to talk freely with the young Nimrod, and taught him the names of all the hounds. It was also no uncommon thing for him, after the fox had been lost the day before, to say, "Well, Master Smith, what became of our fox yesterday?" The lad had always a prompt answer; and as he really had a very quick apprehension, he was often flattered by hearing old Will exclaim, "By jingo, he's right!" But Tom did not confine himself merely to hunting animals; on the contrary, he closely observed them; and having natural artistic talent, he soon began sketching them, thus laying the foundation of the facility which afterwards enabled him to paint the whole Hampshire Hunt at one sitting, as we shall relate by and by, though it must be owned that the sitting was rather a long one.

Tom was still at school when England was threatened with invasion, and Volunteer corps were formed in every quarter in consequence. As at the present day, "cadet corps" were set on foot, though not so named; but the elder school-boys were drilled, and were provided with wooden swords and guns, of which the blades and barrels were handsomely black-leaded; and in order to procure feathers for their hats, the hackle of all the white and red cocks, in Tom's neighbourhood at least, was "appropriated" with or without leave, as might happen. Mr. Smith was a captain in the Bentworth, Shaldon, and Lasham corps; and on Tom quitting school, at the age of seventeen, he was at once appointed an ensign in his father's company, in which he continued until the peace of 1814. He thus acquired a great desire for a military life, and a promise of a commission was obtained for him; but family circumstances afterwards prevented his acceptance of it.

About the close of the war, Mr. Smith built himself a new residence, called Shaldon Lodge, and let the old Manor-house, which he had formerly occupied, to Sir Lawrence Halsted, who resided in it whilst building the mansion now called Theddon Grange, but which he styled Phœnix Lodge, after the ship that he had commanded. Sir Lawrence was often visited by his father-in-law, Sir Edward Pellew, and others of the Pellew family, and an intimacy between them and the Smiths also sprang up. Captain Pownoll Pellew (afterwards the second Lord Exmouth) was a particularly bad shot, but yet was fond of blazing away at the birds; and this gave occasion to Tom Smith to indulge his natural love of fun by hoaxing him. They were out together in Theddon Wood, when a woodcock rose close to the gallant captain, who drew the trigger, and it fell dead. Half frantic with delight,

he dashed forward, picked it up, declaring it
to be the finest bird that ever was seen; then
having most carefully smoothed its feathers,
he placed it almost reverentially in his pocket,
saying how delighted his sister, Lady Halsted,
would be, as it was the first bird he had ever
killed on the wing. Tom professed himself
equally delighted, and urged him to reload his
gun, as woodcocks were often found two together. The captain proceeded to do so, when
he found that his gun had missed fire, and
that it was the report of Tom's gun that he
had mistaken for his own. Terribly indignant,
he tore the bird from his pocket, and hurled
it at Tom's head, stigmatising him as the
greatest humbug he had ever seen. This
was rather unfair, as Tom did not know that
the captain's gun had missed fire, and was
quite willing to give him the credit of the
shot. Tom, indeed, was rather misunderstood
by the Pellews, though he always was on
excellent terms with them, and with Dean Pel-

lew—now, alas! no more—long the only sur-
vivor of the party. The Dean, writing not
long before his own death to him, alluded most
kindly to their youthful sports. Yet even he
made a terrible accusation against his old
friend, quite sufficient to ruin him in the eyes
of sportsmen, which is, that once when they
were shooting in a wood together, he saw a
fox pass; and as Tom's gun had been discharged only the moment before, he thought
that Reynard must have been shot at. Mr.
Smith, after this lapse of time, cannot give an
account of all that he may have done on that
day, whenever it was; but he knows that even
at that age his veneration for a fox was such,
that he thought a man who would shoot one
would shoot his own father. So he has no
hesitation in pleading "not guilty."

On one occasion Sir Edward borrowed a
strong gray horse belonging to Mr. Smith,
and rode it a few miles to call on a relative of
his wife's, who lived at Burkham. The Ad-

miral was a very great weight; and on his
return he complained sadly of the rough ride
he had had, saying, sailor-like, that he "must
be fresh coppered;" but his horse seemed to
have the worst of it, for it fell dead lame, and
had to be turned out into the marshes for some
months.   At last it was found that it had not
been crippled by the twenty stone or so of the
future victor at Algiers, but had been lamed
by a sharp flint, which in due time worked out
at the coronet, between the hair and hoof.

Shortly after this, the premature death of
Mr. Smith entirely altered the prospects of his
eldest son, as he considered it his duty to sacri-
fice his own inclinations in order the better to
assist his widowed mother.   Mrs. Smith was a
woman of extraordinary energy and ability;
but she had twelve children to provide for,
and it was resolved that the eldest should give
up his promised career in the army, and, instead, take charge of the farm, which was an
extensive one.   The friend who had endea-

voured to procure him a commission was Mr.
James Ward, then a very young man, who
was paying his addresses to one of the Misses
Smith. He was a well-known member of the
Hampshire Hunt, and a county magistrate;
which latter position was bestowed on him at
the early age of twenty-one. But though Mr.
Ward could not gratify his friend in one
way, he resolved to do it in another. It was
his custom to make an annual visit to his former guardian at Lyndhurst, taking his three
hunters with him, so as to join the New
Forest hounds. He now pressed Tom to
accompany him, who gladly consented. They
got to Lyndhurst all right; but on the next
day young Ward, full of tender thoughts of
"the girl he had left behind him," changed
his mind, and rushed back to Shaldon, leaving
his three hunters, his first-rate grooms, his
scarlet coat and boots, all unreservedly at the
disposal of his friend Smith. The latter was
now at the height of his ambition: the splen-

did hunter, the first-rate groom, the scarlet coat and boots, seemed almost too good news to be true; but he took care to make good use of them nevertheless, and thus he soon attracted the notice of the master of the hounds, that famous old sportsman, Mr. John Warde, who frequently invited him to dine with him, especially after a good day's sport. The intimacy thus begun endured as long as Mr. Warde's life; he was proud of his pupil, and was often heard to say, when any instance of the prowess of the latter was related in after days, "I entered Tom Smith to hounds."

CHAPTER II.

Farming—Vice-President of the Winchester Agricultural
Show — Fox-hunting — Cricket — Devon Stag-hounds —
Marriage—Residence at Hill House, Hambledon—Visit
to Scotland—Lord Fife's practical jokes—Mr. Owen, of
New Lanark—An unpleasant mistake—Adventure in a
coal-mine—"Out of debt, out of danger."

IT fortunately happened that in the very first
year of his farming Mr. Smith was able to be
of great service to his family by his energy
and good management. Wheat was enor-
mously high at the time of harvest; and
foreseeing that this could not long continue,
he exerted himself as few young men would
have thought of doing to get his crop to
market. A threshing-machine had been employed a year before by Sir Thomas Miller, at
Froyle; but it was no favourite with farmers
or labourers, and nobody, in that part of the

country at least, thought of using it. Mr. Smith, however, being, as will be seen hereafter, of a mechanical turn of mind, satisfied himself of its merits, and ventured on one of his own, which he set to work as soon as the crop was housed. It was of six-horse power, and by employing three sets of men and horses working day and night, he soon had nearly forty loads of wheat threshed out, which sold at from 45*l.* to 48*l.* per load; the price fell before the next harvest to 12*l.* or 13*l.*

About this time Bennet, of Farnham, had invented a hand-machine for sowing turnip and grass seeds in drills; and Mr. Smith desired him to add a long trough of wood to be filled with ashes, so as to be dropped into the drill on the turnip-seed. The improved machine was sent to the Agricultural Exhibition at Winchester, when a prize for the invention was awarded to Mr. Smith, which he handed over to Bennet.

In connection with this Agricultural Exhibition, a proof of Mr. Smith's untiring energy may be related. He was one of the Vice-Presidents, and, of course, it was necessary that he should be at the opening; but he knew how to combine pleasure with business. He was passionately fond of dancing, and was sure to be well received by the ladies. On the evening before the show he rode from his house, near Alton, a distance of eighteen miles, to a ball at Henley Park, near Guildford, and danced until four in the morning. Then he changed his dress, mounted his horse, and rode to Winchester, forty miles off, where he arrived before eleven, the hour for the opening. Neither he nor his horse seemed to have suffered from this. Soon after, he rode over to Mr. Chute, at the Vine. It was a frost, but the old squire had the hounds out. The fox took a line down Freemantle Hill, one of the steepest in that country, followed by the hounds. Although there was a large field, Mr. Smith was soon left alone with them; and when, after riding several miles, the men came up, they found him in the midst of the pack, with the fox in his hands.

Shortly after this he accepted an invitation into Sussex, to witness the last day that the Duke of Richmond's hounds hunted fox, before they went to Swinley to hunt stag, having been made a present of to the Prince Regent. On this day they had a capital run; Mr. Smith was luckily the first in at the death, and took the brush.

His next sport was in Devonshire, where his brother Samuel for ten years held the perpetual curacy of Tiverton. This occasioned him to pay several visits to that country, where he was introduced to Mr. Newton Fellowes, who kept a pack of large foxhounds at Eggesford, and whose cheery voice, "Cover-hoick," when he threw them into cover, can never be forgotten. He also became a member of the cricket-club at Barnstaple; and as he had had some previous experience in Hamp-

shire, he was able to be of service in their
matches with the Teignbridge club. This
caused him to be sought after; and accordingly, when he was one day sailing with his
friend Mr. Fleming, of Stoneham Park, in his
yacht Elizabeth, he received a letter particularly begging him to join his Barnstaple
friends at eleven o'clock next day. The yacht
was then off the Isle of Wight, and it seemed
hardly possible to be in time; but Mr. Smith
resolved to try. He was instantly set on
shore, travelled all night (there were no railways then), and reached Exeter, where a car-
riage-and-four was in waiting with some of the
party. He was just allowed time for a plunge
in the bath at the inn and a cup of tea, and
then repaired to the field. The Barnstaple
party was successful; but many expressed the
opinion that it would have been otherwise if
the Hampshire man had not been there.

Another sport that he enjoyed in Devonshire was otter-hunting, along with Mr.

Treby's hounds; they commenced work at four
in the morning, and he was highly gratified.
He also became acquainted with that keen and
good sportsman, the Rev. J. Russell, who rode
his famed horse Monkey on the day that Sir
Arthur Chichester had a wonderful run with
his stag-hounds. The Devonshire mode of
proceeding is worth description. The stag
was roused by three or four couple of hounds
only, called tufters; the rest of the pack being
kept shut up until the stag broke cover.
Then they were let loose, and, to the surprise
of our Hampshire friend, the whole field, led
by the Rev. Nimrod, instead of trying to be
with the pack, took a line parallel to the
stag, who, with the hounds after him, ran
clean away. Although our friend Smith was
mounted by Sir Arthur on a thorough-bred,
he was obliged to pull up. When, in consequence, he was making his way to shoot with
Mr. Fellowes, at Dulverton, he fell in with
two men in scarlet, with two hounds, going

towards home; they were the Master and the huntsman. The former, on being asked what would become of the hounds, quietly replied, "Oh! they'll find their way back to the kennel in the course of a day or two; this sort of thing often happens." Very likely it did, for it was evidently impossible for any horse in the world to keep with stag-hounds in such runs as that.

Soon after his return from Devonshire Mr. Smith's prospects were changed greatly for the better. He had been requested by a friend to visit a kennel at East Meon, where there was a pack of fox-hounds which were expected to be shortly for sale, in consequence of the death of the owner. On leaving the kennel they met two ladies: one of whom was the clergyman's wife, and a friend of Mr. Smith's family; the other lady was the widow of the Master of Hounds. The usual introductions were followed by an acquaintance, and at the end of the year the lady became

Mrs. Smith. Never was man blessed with a more amiable partner, and if ever pair were, they were honestly entitled to the Dunmow flitch. They resided in the house at East Meon for a few years, and then removed to Hill House, Hambledon.

It may not be received in Kent or Sussex, but it is a fact that in Hampshire the origin of the game of cricket is ascribed to Hambledon; and its old-established club was in full swing when Mr. Smith came to reside there. He accepted the office of secretary; and from the old club-books that thus came into his hands we glean some curious particulars, which afford strong presumption in favour of the claim. The game, it seems, was at first practised with one stump only, then with two, and lastly with three. For some years after Mr. Smith's connection with the club, there was suspended from the roof of the club-house, on Windmill Down, an old worm-eaten bat, more resembling Hercules' club than any

thing to be seen at the present day, and
which was in high estimation among the
members. Unluckily, after a club dinner, a
young member who had his grog on board,
jumped on the table, and ran off with the
precious relic, to have, as he said, " one hit ;"
the hit shattered it to atoms, when the culprit
had to make a speedy retreat, or unpleasant
consequences would certainly have resulted
from the outraged feelings of the spectators.

The Hambledon men were all cricketers ;
but a few names must be specially mentioned.
Foremost among them was Mr. Hale, the
owner of Windmill Down ; and Mr. Bonham
of Petersfield, Colonel King, and Messrs. Richards and Butler were constant attendants
at the matches which Mr. Smith exerted himself to get up. He was an enthusiast about
the game ; and having often played at Lord's
with the Marylebone Club, he was well acquainted with Mr. William Ward, and generally prevailed on him to attend the Ham-

bledon matches. Mr. Ward in one match at
Lord's scored 272 runs. On one occasion
Mr. Smith was opposed to him at a match in
the Isle of Wight. Ward was bowling, and
Smith hit the ball back nearly straight; Ward
attempted to catch, but could only reach the
ball with the tip of one finger, which was
broken back flat on his hand, and he could
play no more that season.

The Hambledon club were tolerably successful in their matches, and whether successful
or not, the little place was always a scene of
gaiety on such occasions, as it was Mr. Smith's
custom to invite all the strangers to his house,
and the evening was usually finished up with
a dance. One match played is worth record-
ing. The Hambledons had to go in the last
innings against nearly 200 runs. Mr. Smith
held his bat during the fall of nine wickets,
when seventy-two runs were to be got. The
tenth player, Colonel Hogg, having left the
ground, believing it to be a lost game, the

Sussex gentlemen told Mr. Smith to call in any other in his place. Mr. T. Butler, of Berry Lodge, then brought in his bat, when these two players got the seventy-two runs and won the game.

Another sociable institution of Hambledon was a whist-club, consisting of six or seven families, which met at their respective houses once a week. The cricket-club was given up, and Windmill Down brought into cultivation. Mr. Smith left Hambledon shortly after; but the kindness and hospitality that he enjoyed there can never be forgotten by him. But this is rather anticipating the course of events.

After a few months passed at Hambledon, improving the house, &c., Mr. Smith went to London with his wife for a short time early in the spring. Having looked in at Tattersall's, he bought a brown horse which belonged to Colonel Bowater, and was reported to be a capital hunter. This induced him to go with the royal pack of stag-hounds, along

with an old Marlow friend, Mr. John Brook,
of whose bold riding much had been said.
The consequence was rather unpleasant. Mr.
Smith's ardour was roused; he had no idea of
being cut out in horsemanship, and he so
urged on his poor steed that it died on the
way home, and was disposed of to a knacker
for a guinea; a bargain this, which enabled
him to tell his wife with a clear conscience
that he had sold him, though of course the
particulars oozed out under cross-examination.
This incident is mentioned to warn young
sportsmen never to hunt or ride hard a horse
that is fat and out of condition.

When in London, Mr. Smith's good friend
Mr. G. Taylor procured for him from the
Earl of Fife permission to shoot grouse, and
to fish for salmon in the Deveron. In his
way to Scotland he managed to be at Edinburgh when King George IV. arrived there,
which was in August 1822. At the request
of Lady Jane Taylor, who was the wife of

Major Taylor and sister of the Earl of Fife, he made a sketch from her window of the arrival of the king in his yacht, which her ladyship carefully preserved. He also saw Sir Walter Scott busily engaged in marshalling the Highlanders preparatory to their taking part in the royal reception.

Leaving Edinburgh, he rented a nice house in the town of Keith for two months, and commenced salmon-fishing. His first attempt was not successful, as after hooking a fine salmon, and bringing it on to the shingle after half an hour's play, it gave a sudden spring and escaped, carrying a good part of the line with it. This was a lesson, and he used a gaff for the future. But he had not much time to give to salmon, as it was now the grouse season; so he bought two good pointers, and had excellent sport with them, although his greatest bag was only thirty-six brace. These he sent to his friends in England, packed in layers, in a box surrounded by hops; and they arrived all safe and good, although there were then no railways. Beside these, he killed a few black-cock, but only one ptarmigan.

Part of the time in Scotland was passed at Duff House, the seat of the Earl of Fife; a nobleman whose peculiarities were generally amusing, but on one occasion proved anything but pleasant. His lordship asked Mr. Smith to go with him to see a wild boar, which he kept in an outhouse. Arrived at the spot, two ladders were placed against the wall, which my lord and his visitor ascended; but the instant Mr. Smith reached the top he found the boar, with open jaws and enormous tusks, grinning horribly close to his face, and making frantic efforts to seize him. The "joke" was, that Lord Fife carried hid under his coat a whip with which he " touched up" the boar; and the wonder was that a fall backwards did not occur.

After leaving Duff House, Mr. and Mrs.

Smith went to Lanark to see the falls of the
Clyde. On the following day, which was
Sunday, they received an invitation from Mr.
and Mrs. Owen, of New Lanark, to spend the
day with them at their much-talked-of establishment. Prompted by curiosity, they went,
and were courteously received. But they
soon found that Sunday was not observed in
the customary manner here; for Mr. Owen
took them into a large room, where about one
hundred boys and girls were assembled, who
by his desire sang "Scots, wha hae," &c. &c.
Mrs. Smith observing one particularly nice,
clever-looking girl, remarked that she would
be glad to take her into her service; upon
which the philosophic Mr. Owen grew out-
rageously indignant, declaring that none of
his young people were ever intended for the
degradation of household service; and he re-
peated this so vehemently, that his visitors
returned with speed to their inn. Before
leaving Scotland they visited Dundee, where

they made the acquaintance of Mr. Kean,
with whom and his wife they visited
Glammis Castle, and some other celebrated
places.

Some time after this Mr. Smith went into
Cheshire, on a visit to a cousin of his, who
had married the Rev. Giles Peel, a cousin of
the second Sir Robert Peel, and incumbent of
Ince. From their house he went one day to
Sandywell Head to see the Cheshire hounds.
He staid till it was nearly dark looking over
the hounds, especially the clever lot of unentered ones, which were equal in point of
size and muscle to any in the kingdom. He
had a good distance to walk back to his inn,
and did not arrive till quite late. He retired
at once to his room, but was disturbed by a
great noise of footsteps passing and repassing
his door; and when he awoke in the morning
he heard the same, with the addition of whis-
pering and low speaking. When he came down
to breakfast, he noticed the boots followed

him into the room, and was at once joined
by the landlord, who asked a series of ques-
tions as to where he had come from, and where
he was going to, in a tone that grew more and
more impertinent, until at last Mr. Smith lost
his temper, and exclaimed, "What the—is all
that to you?" At last came the explanation.
A highway robbery had been committed in
the neighbourhood the night before, and the
good people of the inn fancied that their guest
might possibly be the offender, as he came to
the house so late. Laughing and storming by
turns, Mr. Smith exhibited an envelope addressed to Mr. Peel, on which that gentleman
had jotted down his route to the Kennels;
and now it was the turn of the poor host to
make a thousand abject apologies for his in-
jurious suspicions.

During his visit to Ince, Mr. Smith had a
very narrow escape from loss of life to himself
and others, which may well be related as a
caution. He had a desire to see a coal-mine;

and Mr. Gibbons, the owner of one of the deepest in the neighbourhood, formed a party for the purpose, and accompanied them himself. When they arrived at the bottom, some hundreds of feet below the surface, a light was placed in the hand of each, and they proceeded along the passages. At length Mr. Smith noticed a dark hole some three or four feet wide above his head, and he was in the act of raising his lamp to see more clearly what it was, when he received a severe blow on the arm, which brought both hand and lamp to the ground, accompanied by a frantic exclamation, "Oh! heavens!" His consternation may be imagined when he was told that the hole was filled with gas, which the raising of his lamp only a few inches higher would have ignited, when the destruction of the pit and all in it would have been the work of a moment.

Another danger which Mr. Smith has escaped is the danger of debt; and he is ever ready to maintain that he has escaped this danger and its penalties, owing to "a word spoken in season" by Colonel Johnston, his brother-in-law. The Colonel and Mr. Smith were going out to ride one day, when a fish-hawker came up, and some of his ware was purchased; after which the party prepared to start, when the Colonel said, "Smith, the fish is not paid for." The hawker cried, "Oh! sir, I know Mr. Smith well enough; he will pay me another day." But this did not suit Colonel Johnston's ideas, who took money from his pocket, and would have paid the trifle, but that Mr. Smith anticipated him. When the man was gone, the Colonel asked, "Smith, how could you bear to put it in the power of such a fellow as that to say that you owed him a shilling even for a day?" The reproof went home, and under any difficulties "ready-money payment" has ever since been the practice of Mr. Smith; to which he attributes his success in life, and which cannot be

too earnestly impressed on every man, particularly if he ventures on so troublesome and
uncertain an occupation as that of master of
hounds.

CHAPTER III.

Sport in the New Forest—Sir Bellingham Graham—The
horse General—Mr. Smith becomes Master of the Hambledon hounds—Unpromising beginning—Extraordinary
run into Sussex—Mr. Smith's picture of the H. H., with
sixty-five likenesses—Visit to the Quorn—An unexpected
honour.

IN the spring of 1823 Mr. Smith took his two
hunters to Lyndhurst for a week's hunting in
the New Forest, which at that time was annually visited by many masters of hounds
and celebrated sportsmen. Among them was
Sir Bellingham Graham, whom he had known
formerly when a cadet at the Military College,
Great Marlow, and had frequently met, with
Sir Godfrey Webster, dining at his uncle's,
Mr. Wethered. He well recollects seeing
these two young baronets, with their orange-
coloured hunting-coats, riding to meet the old
Berkeley hounds—that colour being the uni-

form of that hunt—since changed to scarlet
with black collar, and silver fox on it. A
large house called Remnants was at that time
used for the college: it was afterwards purchased by Mr. Wethered, and converted into
a most charming residence. This gentleman
left by will 1000*l.* to provide for a second
sermon on every Sabbath day.

On this occasion Sir Bellingham rode a
famous horse, Beeswax. One day, when the
chase was across the New Park at Lyndhurst,
Mr. Nichol, the Master, called to the baronet,
and told him that he must come to the gate, as
they had a deer-fence before them. Sir Bellingham only shook his head, and went on
with the hounds straight to the palings, which
the pack was getting over or through as they
might. Mr. Smith wished to see how one of
the noted hard riders would act in such a
case; he therefore kept close; and when the
baronet's horse went over the fence, he went
over it also, and the ditch beyond, all right;

LONDON. CHAPMAN & HALL. 193, PICCADILLY 1864.

DAY & SON, LIMITED. LITH.

SIR BELLINGHAM GRAHAM AND T. SMITH RIDING OVER THE PARK PALING
AT FOXLEES LYNDHURST NEW FOREST.

but Beeswax came down on his chest; however, he soon got up again, and both horsemen came up with the hounds before they had killed their fox. When Mr. Nichol and the rest of the field arrived, Sir Bellingham told them what had occurred, and offered at once to give 250 guineas for Mr. Smith's horse, which was called the General, and had cost but forty-five guineas three mo ↄ before. Mr. Smith, however, preferred to keep his steed; and some of his performances will be related hereafter.

Some time after this Mr. Smith had an adventure in the New Forest, which he made the subject of a spirited picture,—one included in the Loan Exhibition at Southampton in 1866.

The royal stag-hounds met that day at Stoney Cross, intending to take a particular old stag which had been doing mischief in the cottage gardens. It was found lying by the keepers, was roused; and the hounds being shortly after laid on, they went at a most

awful pace, which it appeared impossible for
horses to maintain. Mr. Smith allowed every
horse to pass him, being 500 at the least, and
followed them quietly, until he saw them bear-
ing to the right, when he rode across, and was
shortly first, instead of last. He kept his eye
on the leading hounds, and they ran into a
patch of bushes and among trees. He keeping
outside, saw the same hounds leading as usual
into this covert, and he continued with them,
only two couple going away. He hallooed as
loud as he could; but no other hounds came
after them, and only four or five men. They
ran straight across the forest for eight or ten
miles, and into an enclosure called the Frenches,
where he followed; but he found the other
men at the end of the enclosure, who must
have headed the stag, as the then only two
hounds came to a check; and after making a
cast forward without success, he brought them
to the spot where they had been checked. On
riding into some high fern, he saw the stag

LONDON, CHAPMAN & HALL, 193, PICCADILLY 1866.

DAY & SON, LIMITED LITH

TAKING THE STAG WITH ONLY TWO OF THE ROYAL STAG HOUNDS.

lying on the ground, with his horns flat on his back, like a rabbit in her form. Mr. Smith whipped him up, when he broke away out of the enclosure, and ran for four or five miles, with the two hounds close to his haunches. Luckily Mr. Smith's horse jumped over the palings; and so he kept in sight of them until the stag ran into a stream of water, and stood in it, defying the hounds; he gave one of them a kick, but being in the water, it was not hurt. Mr. Smith remained for nearly an hour sitting on the bank and hallooing, until a forest-keeper came, whom he sent to inform Davis, the huntsman. Shortly after, one of the whippers-in came up, and directly jumped off his horse close to the stag, which then quietly trotted out of the water. Mr. Smith begged the whipper-in to mount his horse, saying that the stag was not much distressed, as his mouth was shut. The man said, "That only proves that he's done;" and so it proved; for when the stag had gone about 100 yards, he quietly trotted back again into the water, and remained there until Davis came up with the hounds and the whole field. Lord Rosslyn, on arriving, inquired who had gone on with the two hounds. No one answered; and seeing Mr. Smith sitting on the bank, he uncourteously said—

"Mr. Smith, you must have been the person."

On his pleading guilty, his lordship said—

"You ought to have stopped them."

"Stop them!" was the reply; "I might as well try to stop the Thames. I had enough to do to keep within sight of them."

"Then, sir, if you had been a sportsman, you would have stopped them."

To which Mr. Smith replied—

"When I want a character, I shall not come to your lordship for it."

The stag was shortly taken out, and his horns sawn off, which were offered to Mr. Smith; but he refused to receive them, after what Lord Rosslyn had said. The stag was taken to Swinley.

When Mr. Shard gave up the Hambledon hounds, Mr. Smith, at the request of friends, agreed to take the management. He therefore purchased Mr. Shard's pack, and kept them at Mr. Goodlad's, at Hill Place, where he also lived, until it was required by the owner. Mr. Shard, it should be said, had hunted that country, after Sir Bellingham Graham and Mr. Osbaldeston had each had it for half a season only. No time was lost in procuring huntsmen and whippers-in. Old Will James was kept as kennel huntsman, and John Major offered his services, which were accepted. John had formerly belonged to the Hampshire hounds; but he had lately been in France, where he had imbibed a taste for brandy that made him almost useless. He only killed one fox in the first six weeks; and on then being told at cover side that he must kill one that day, he coolly handed the

horn over to the Master, saying he had better
hunt the hounds himself. John was of course
sent home, and Mr. Smith was left to his own
resources. A fox was shortly after found in
North Coppice, which, after a ring or two in
cover, broke away; all appeared prosperous,
until the hounds were running on the opposite
side of a wide hedge-row, when on a sudden
they stopped, and seemed to have killed their
fox, to the great joy of the new huntsman,
which, however, was soon turned into grief;
for when he rushed through the hedge-row to
take up the fox, he found that his hounds had
killed a poor sheep. He at once believed himself ruined for life as a huntsman; and after
rating and flogging the hounds so furiously as
to bring all the field to the spot, he took them
home. The Rev. G. Richards, and that kind
good man Mr. Butler, rode part of the way
with him, and endeavoured to console him,
assuring him, from their experience, that such
an event was not very unusual early in the

season and with young hounds, and telling
him that they would make it all right with
the owner of the sheep. On reaching the kennel, John Major, the discarded huntsman, first
met the hounds, and said in a dissatisfied
tone—

" I see you have had blood to-day."

"Yes," was the only reply; which sent
him away as miserable as the master, until
he learnt the real state of the case, when he
became jolly enough. In the course of the
evening the shepherd came (no doubt sent by
good Mr. Butler) to thank the unlucky huntsman for having killed a poor giddy sheep that
had given him " a mort o' trouble." Even
this well-meant device did not comfort poor
Mr. Smith, and he went to bed only to be
tormented with frightful dreams, in which his
hounds appeared to be hunting everything but
foxes. However, he determined to give them
one more trial; and although with a doubtful
heart, he took them to the place of meeting the

next hunting-day. He judiciously kept his doubts to himself, and men who expected to find him downcast saw him apparently in his usual high spirits, which was soon really the case, as he killed his fox that day after a good run. The incident was soon forgotten by all but himself: but he turned it to use; for it determined him never to let the hounds be out of his sight when in chase.

Notwithstanding the misadventure of their first day, the Hambledon pack turned out a good one. They had, as "Nimrod" allowed, one of the most extraordinary runs on record. The meet was at Stanstead, which was at that time a neutral covert with them and Colonel G. Wyndham, whose hounds met the same day at Allsworth Bridge, only a mile off. This was inconveniently near, and at Colonel Wyndham's request, made through Mr. Bingham Newland, Mr. Smith retired, leaving Stanstead for the Colonel. The Hambledons found in the Markwells, between two and three o'clock, ran up wind to Gravel Hill, where the fox was headed, and viewed at the turnpike road near Highdown Wood. He turned short back down wind, through and across Harting Down, Up Park, and over the Sussex Downs, through West Dean woods and close to Colonel Wyndham's kennel at the Drove, through the large Williams' wood, keeping in the roads in the wood throughout. The pack, therefore, certainly did not change their fox, who was evidently running for some point, probably an earth; but this being the Colonel's hunting-day, it most likely was stopped. He then took a line at an awful pace over the downs, sinking the hill near to Petworth, and after crossing that deep bottom by Burton Park to Graffham Hill, crossed the London and Chichester road, and ran again over the downs to a large wood on the right, where the hounds got up to him. He was often seen almost among them, and nothing could have saved him, only just at this crisis a

E

man outside the wood unluckily hallooed them on to a fresh fox away over the open down. It was impossible to get up to the hounds until they had got into Potcombe Wood, when it was getting dark, or they would have been taken back to the wood where they had left their beaten fox, which had been so nearly killed that one man got off his horse believing such to be the case.

It was now time to think of home, which was not less than forty miles off, and there was scarcely light enough to count the hounds. When this was done, it appeared that two were missing. The horn was accordingly blown two or three times, and a halloo was heard at a distance in reply. Shortly after one of Colonel Wyndham's men rode up with a message from his master, inviting Mr. Smith to take up his quarters with him for the night, the pack, &c. of course being included in the invitation. They reached the Drove between eight and nine o'clock; and after he had seen to his hounds, Mr. Smith sat down to dinner in his host's clothes, well pleased to be spared the long ride home that night. Shortly after dinner the Colonel left the room; and when he returned he said that he could not help going to see how a pack of hounds looked after such an extraordinary long and hard run. He said that when he went into the lodging-room with a lantern, all the hounds jumped off the benches with their sterns over their backs, as if ready to start off home, thus proving their stoutness and condition. Before breakfast next morning the Colonel wrote an account of this run to his father, Lord Egremont, which he read to his visitor, in order that it might be corrected, if needful. It finished thus: "If Smith had found his fox at my kennel-door, which they passed near, it would have been one of the best and straightest runs I ever saw; but they had come when there at least seventeen miles!"

The account of this extraordinary run must

prove to Masters of Hounds that they must keep nearly as many hounds to hunt three days as to hunt four. At this time the subscription was under 600*l.*, and therefore only thirty or thirty-two couple were kept in the Hambledon pack. To make up a proper pack of eighteen couple, Mr. Smith was obliged to include four or five couple that had hunted two days before, generally the youngest or freshest. This great run was on a Monday, and on the Wednesday he was forced to take out four couple that had been engaged in it. There was an immense field from Sussex, who came to hear the true account of the Monday's performance; and he ventured to tell them all that these four couple would be soon far behind the rest, if they ran at all. This was fulfilled to the very letter. In fact, if foxhounds are worked too often, that is, before they have had time to get quite fresh again, they will lose the dash of foxhounds, and be nothing better than a pack of harriers.

We have said in an early chapter that Mr. Smith had a talent for painting, and this he displayed about this time by producing a picture which contained sixty-five portraits of men and horses belonging to the Hampshire Hunt. It happened in this way. He was riding to Hinton House, the place of meet, along with Mr. G. Richards, when, from the opposite hill, he saw the whole party grouped before the house. It was a dull frosty day; but a gleam of sunshine suddenly broke through, and it occurred to him that this was a good subject for a picture. At a glance he took in the whole scene; and he retained it so thoroughly in his mind, that though he was late home after the run to Allington, he commenced his work immediately after dinner. He worked on, hour after hour, until five o'clock the next morning, and then he had finished the picture, which now hangs in the dining-room at Fir Hill. Almost incredible as it may seem, he never once touched a single figure of man or horse again ; and yet so exact are the likenesses, that every one can be, and has been, identified. The Hunt wished to have the picture engraved, but Mr. Smith declined such an honour; it was, however, engraved after all, without his knowledge.

After the hunting season Mr. Smith again went to Scotland. During his absence from home, Lady Gage called and requested to see the picture, as the likenesses of her two sons and Admiral Gage were in it. It was brought to her in her carriage, when she drove off with it, leaving a message, that, by the wish of the Hunt, she would take it to London to have it engraved. This message, by some oversight, was not forwarded to Mr. Smith, and thus a little surprise was prepared for him at Melton, where he stayed on his way back from Scotland. He there found Ferneley the artist busy with a picture of all the men and horses belonging to the Quorn Hunt. He asked permission to see this, which was readily granted; and in the course of conversation the artist asked him his reason for wishing to see it. He replied, that he had never seen a picture of a whole Hunt before. Ferneley replied, "That is very likely, for there never was but one of a whole Hunt ever painted." Mr. Smith inquired where that one could be seen, and was told that if he would go, when in London, to Watson's in Vere-street, he would there see a picture containing the likenesses of all the men belonging to the Hampshire Hunt, which had been painted by a Mr. Smith, and was then being engraved by Turner. Ferneley added that he had taken other artists to see the picture, and they had all agreed it was the first attempt that had ever been made to paint a whole Hunt, and this had led him to undertake the picture he had then in hand. This was flattering news for his visitor; and he has since seen the example that he thus set followed with regard to several other Hunts.

After seeing Ferneley's picture, Mr. Smith

went over to Quorndon, where Sir Bellingham
Graham, his old acquaintance, was then Master of Hounds.   On the following day they
rode together to the first regular meet at
Kirby Gate.   Mr. Smith was mounted on the
General, for which Sir Bellingham had offered
250 guineas; but he told the baronet that
these Leicestershire hard riders rather fright-
ened him.

"Never mind," was the answer; "you'll
get along with that horse; besides, after the
first five minutes you'll see only ten or twelve
of them with the hounds;" which turned out
to be the case.   To his surprise, when the
hounds were running across a large pasture,
these men turned to the left away from them;
but he, seeing what he took to be only a
common fence, rode straight on.   It was a
fence, to be sure; but on the other side was
an awfully wide and deep ditch, which his
horse could not clear.   Instead, he performed
a complete somerset, and fell on his back,

H DEL.

LONDON CHAPMAN & HALL 193 PICCADILLY 1866

DAY & SON. LIMITED. LITH.

AN AWFUL LEAP WITH QUORN HOUNDS

sending his rider headlong before him, to the great amusement of the Quorners. Luckily neither man nor horse was much hurt; they were soon on the go again, and joined the rest. After a severe run the fox was viewed close before the hounds, under a high upright spiked gate, which Sir Bellingham and Sir James Musgrave tried to lift off the hooks. Whilst they were thus employed Mr. Smith came up, when the General carried him over the pales beside the gate, and he was the only one in the field when the fox was killed. Presently Sir Bellingham and a few others came up, when the baronet offered the brush to Mr. Smith, saying—

"Tell the Hampshire lads that I can kill a fox here, though I didn't kill many among them."

Sir Francis Burdett was present, and seeing the brush in Mr. Smith's hand, he, in the most quiet and kindly manner, advised him not to take it, saying—

" We never do it in this county."

Mr. Smith thanked him for the hint, and told him what message Sir Bellingham had given him. Sir Francis never forgot the General, and repeatedly offered tô purchase him at any price, until Mr. Smith put an end to it by saying that he would take nothing less than an annuity of 100*l.* for life; and even after that Sir Francis was often heard to express his regret that he had not been able to obtain the horse.

Mr. Smith had a somewhat similar accident afterwards, whilst hunting his own hounds, the Pytchley. They came suddenly to an awkward fence, namely, a single rail on a bank between two ditches. Although two or three of the " hard riders" were before him, they very politely allowed him to pass them; and as the rail was but a low one, he thought it practicable, and rode at it. Unfortunately he was not mounted on the General, or it might have been all right. As it was, his horse fell into the wide ditch on the far side, and his rider, as soon as he could gather himself up, had to pull him out by the tail. He remounted, and shortly after overtook the hounds; alone, before any of the rest of the field came up, as they had made a long *détour* to have the benefit of a gate. A day or two after this, Mr. Isted, one of the hard riders, and who was also a clever draftsman, was amusing some of the party with a sketch that he had made of this fall, and in due time it was handed to the subject of it. Mr. Smith remarked that he had forgotten one incident, which he would supply ; and taking a pencil, he added a portrait of a horseman, who bore a tolerable resemblance to Mr. Isted, gallopping along with others away from the hounds and making for the gate. The sketch thus completed is probably still in Mr. Isted's portfolio.

During this visit to Sir Bellingham Mr. Smith had the pleasure of preventing a duel,

which at one time seemed imminent. Information came one day, after dinner, that
Lord Anson had run a fox to ground in the
Quorndon country, and then, contrary to custom, had had it dug out. Sir Bellingham
fell into a towering rage, and on the instant
wrote a challenge to his lordship. With difficulty Mr. Smith prevailed on the baronet
not to send it off instanter, but to take it
with him to the meet next day, and abide
by the judgment of the Hunt. This was,
that if any insult was meant, it was not to
Sir B., but to the whole Hunt; but that great
allowance was to be made for so young a
Master of Hounds as his lordship, and that
a letter of remonstrance was all that was
called for. Rather reluctantly Sir Bellingham
gave up the "affair," and he was repaid by
a capital run, with blood of fox instead of
a lord at the end of it.

On his way home Mr. Smith paid a visit to
Great Marlow. Hearing that the royal stag-

hounds met close by, at Maidenhead thicket, he
joined them; and when they were taking the
stag out of a small stream, he sat down on the
wall of the bridge, holding his horse. He was
accosted by an elegant and high-bred lady,
who was also on the bridge, and who made the
remark that he did not appear to take much
interest in such hunting; to which he replied
that he did not, for he had just returned
from hunting with the Quorn hounds, where
he had had capital sport. The lady replied that
she had lately received a letter from a friend,
whose hounds hunted the adjoining country
to the Quorn, who stated that his pack had
had better sport than the Quorn. She then
asked if he had ever been further north; to
which he replied that previous to the hunting season he had been on a visit to Lord
Fife at Duff House, for salmon-fishing in the
Deveron, and grouse-shooting over his lordship's moors, which were the most extensive
in the north; to which the lady quickly re-

plied: "No, not so extensive as my father's, the Duke of Gordon."

This discovery of his companion's rank did not, however, put an end to their conversation. He led his horse towards Marlow, which proved to be the lady's road home: she walked beside him, conversing most affably; and when they arrived opposite her house, she kindly invited him to enter and refresh himself and his horse. He learnt afterwards that this lady was the Duchess of Manchester.

Whilst Mr. Smith resided at Hill Place he had the pleasure of a visit from Lord Erroll, when an amusing incident occurred. A day or two after his arrival Mr. Smith was told by his footman that my lord's valet was dissatisfied with his accommodation. He had, he said, been accustomed to his bottle of port every day. Mr. Smith asked my lord if such was the case. The reply was:

"Well, I suppose it is, since he says so;

but I never knew it before. But I'll settle
the fellow. I don't want much attendance,
so I'll send him to the nearest public-house
to board; I'll promise he won't drink a bottle
of *their* port."

To the infinite disgust of " my lord's gentleman," this was carried out; and when the
visit ended his master took him back with
him rather chapfallen.

CHAPTER IV.

The Hambledon pack increased—A perilous adventure—
Anecdote of Lord Palmerston—Accidents—Hard riding—
Removal to Swanmere—Death of Mrs. Smith—Society
at Exton—Sir Joseph Yorke and others—Visit to London
—Resigns the Hambledon Hounds.

In Mr. Smith's second season the Hambledon
pack was increased to forty couple; not so the
subscription. A run or two with them may
be related.

It is held by many sportsmen that foxes
which run to ground shortly after being found
are bad, and only fit to be dug out and killed.
Mr. Smith's experience has taught him that
this is an error, and that the oldest and best
foxes will do it on good scenting days—that is,
on days which they know to be such, though
their pursuers may not. On one occasion a
fox was found at Allington; and Mr. Smith
at once sent off the whipper-in to see if the

large earth was stopped just beyond Dummer's coppice by the meadows. After a short ring or two, the fox ran straight to this earth, and the hounds began scratching and trying to get in. Mr. Smith, supposing it had not been stopped, was for the moment very angry; but he soon saw the sticks that the whipper-in had thrust in, and jumping again on his horse, he galloped with the hounds to the end of the wood, where they hit off the scent, and had the finest run possible of fifteen miles before they killed their fox, near the village of West Meon. It was a very fine old fellow. Colonel Greenwood, who alone had kept him company across the dirty Durley country, will recollect Mr. Smith saying, when he had the fox in his hands, "Now I don't care if I never kill another fox;" so good did he consider this run to have been, which was afforded by a fox that would have gone to ground in ten minutes if he could.

In Hampshire it rarely happens that it is

F

necessary to cross wide rivers; but the following good run with blood would have been lost,
had not two men swum across a considerable
river.

On this occasion the Hambledon hounds
met at St. Margaret's, near Titchfield, found
on Mr. Delmé's rough ground, and shortly ran
to the wide river between Titchfield and the
Southampton Water. The bridge was a mile
and a half distant; and therefore Mr. Smith
swam his horse across close after the hounds,
as did also Captain Yorke. When about half-
way across they found their horses sinking,
with only their heads out of water. They
therefore slipped off their backs and swam to
the shore, when the General turned down the
stream, and swam strongly, as if going out to
Spithead; but seeing nothing but water and
boats before him, he changed his mind, tacked
about as he passed a shallow creek, and stuck
his fore feet firmly into the muddy bank.
Captain Yorke's horse followed him to the

T. SMITH AND CAPTAIN YORKE SWIMMING ACROSS THE RIVER BELOW THE FALL.

LONDON. CHAPMAN & HALL, 193. PICCADILLY 1866.

DAY & SON. LIMITED. LITH.

shore. In a short time the whipper-in (who
with the rest had gone round by the bridge)
arrived, and gave the Master his horse. Mr.
Smith and the Captain then dashed off after
the hounds, and killed their fox near Titchfield common, whilst the whipper-in was
getting poor General out of the mud. There
were some carriages on the common, and the
fox was given to the hounds close to them.
One of the company asked Mr. Smith whether
he was not very cold and wet. To which he
replied, "Neither, but I have some water in
my boots;" and holding up his foot, the water
poured out as from a bucket, and steaming as
if from a tea-kettle. This was in the depth of
winter.

Whenever the hounds hunted in the neighbourhood of South Stoneham, Mr. Fleming
made a point of inviting Mr. Smith to pass
the preceding night at his hospitable mansion.
On one occasion there was a fancy ball at
the house, and the amiable hostess promised to

open the ball with him, on condition that he
would wear a Scotch dress. He did so; but
when the time came, he found the dance was to
be the galop, which he had never practised, nor
even heard of. It was too late to hold back
then; so he went to work, trusting to the
chapter of accidents. In a minute his partner
cried with a laugh, "Why, you don't know
the galop!" "No," he replied; "only in the
hunting field." Nevertheless, he found the
time so well marked by the music that he
proved an apt pupil, and ere the dance was
over Mrs. Fleming said, "Now you do it as
well as any of them."

At Mr. Fleming's he often had the pleasure
of meeting Lord Palmerston; of whom, as a
sportsman, an anecdote may be related. His
lordship was in the field one day, when a fox
was found at Bittern. Reynard ran straight
to the water at Bursledon, but did not cross;
instead, he turned short back by Botley coverts
to Bittern, where he ran to ground, with the

hounds actually close to his brush. All the horses had had enough, and all the field left immediately except Lord Palmerston, who appeared anxious that the fox should be got out, saying that the hounds deserved to have him. He was told that it would be a long job, as the soil was sandy, and the fox could dig as fast as the men could. "Never mind," was the reply; "I will stay and help to the end." His horse was accordingly sent with the rest to a farm-stable, and all hands dug away as long as daylight lasted; then lanterns were got; and at a quarter to eleven the fox was got at, after which the future Premier had a ride of fourteen miles in the dark to Broadlands. The explanation of his anxiety was, that his horse was entered for the Hampshire Hunt cup, to qualify for which it was necessary that he should have been in at the death of three foxes—and this made the third.

Lord Palmerston, as is well known, permitted, or rather encouraged, his friends to cor-

respond with him on any topic of public interest; and Mr. Smith often availed himself
of the privilege. His suggestions were always most kindly received, and it was quite
evident from the answers that they had been
attentively weighed. One matter that he
urged on his lordship was the following. He
had seen letters from officers in India, from
which it appeared that the growth of tea was
being greatly extended there; and he submitted that if this was encouraged by the
Government, it might be as well to be prepared for ill-will on the part of the Chinese,
which might lead them to give assistance to
the Russians in their designs on India. This
assistance he thought might take the shape of
allowing Russian forces to pass through their
territory, or at all events to be advantageously
stationed on their western frontier. To meet
this contingency, he suggested the formation
of military colonies in the high and healthy
regions bordering on Thibet, which would at

once serve as a reward to time-expired soldiers, and so keep the pension-list within moderate bounds, and also as convalescent dépôts for invalids. Lord Palmerston replied, that the suggestion was good in itself, but he thought that, from increase of population in Great Britain, all the tea that could be raised in India would be consumed without causing such a falling off in the demand as might alarm or offend the Chinese.

The Hambledon country is an easy one to cross, except the dirty Durley part of it; yet if a man will ride over gates, whether fastened or unfastened, he may get a fall. Mr. Smith has had experience of this, and has broken more bones than most men who still keep in the saddle; indeed, as he says, he considers "he has reduced falling to a science," he has had so much of it; but still he thinks the best use that he can put his experience to is to give a few hints that, if attended to, may make falls rather less serious than they are. His first

broken bone he got in the following way. He
was, during a run, riding out of a farmyard
where the manure was knee-deep, and his horse
hit the unfastened gate before his hind legs
were fairly over; the gate swung open, and
caught the horse's leg between the two upper
bars; down went his rider, and broke his col-
lar-bone. Though in great pain, he managed
to lift the gate off the hooks, and thus saved
his horse's leg; but the effort gave his own
broken bone a terrible wrench. He was taken
into the farm-house, and had a glass of vinegar
—his constant practice in such cases—and was
sent home. This may be a useful hint; for
though he cannot explain how it acts, he
knows that he, and others too, have found it
most beneficial. In a fortnight he rode to see
the hounds, with his arm bound firmly to his
side. This accident should be a caution to
young men to "look before they leap," and to
see whether a gate opens to or from them. He
ought to have done so himself; but the fact is,

that the gate opened on to Winter's Hill common, where cattle are turned out, and it was therefore not hung in the usual way. However, there are other obstacles than oddly-hung gates to be met with in Hampshire; and one of the most extraordinary escapes that Mr. Smith ever heard of happened to a member of the Hambledon. Mr. Barkworth, who was one of their hardest riders, when in chase went full tilt at a low part of a hedge near Basing Park, when, wonderful to relate, he fell flat on his face, and his horse disappeared; it had fallen down a draw-hole seventy feet deep, whence chalk had been drawn for dressing the land. Of course the horse was killed, but his rider did not lose his nerve as well as his steed. Another member of the Hunt was a very noted hard rider; this was Sir J. C. Jervoise, of Idsworth. Many men will ride over fences, but very few would ride down a steep hill like him; indeed he was never known to turn from anything. On one

occasion he rode down that terrible hill opposite Duncumb Wood—of course it was half
gallop, half slide—and when he got to the
bottom, he found that his horse had torn off
three of his shoes. Sir Jervoise would assuredly go in the first flight in the Pytchley
country.

A lady also occasionally hunted with these
hounds, whose nerve had been proved in a
most extraordinary way—Miss M—d. When
on a visit at Holywell, and riding with the
Hambledon hounds in full cry across Waltham Chase, a gentleman's horse in front of
the huntsman and this lady made a complete
somersault when crossing a shallow water-
course, and the rider fell stunned and unable
to move for a second or two. When they saw
him move, and try to rise up, they left him,
the lady laughingly saying, "I really thought
he was killed;" which induced her companion
to say, "Your nerve is extraordinary !" &c.
This remark brought from the lady, when

they next met, the following relation :—
When residing in a town in Italy, or elsewhere abroad, she was suddenly awakened one
night by seeing a man come into her room,
who immediately fell on his knees, praying
that she would listen to him for a moment.
He then told her that she could save him from
destruction, if she would suffer him to remain
there a very short time. On hearing this, she
allowed him to recount his story, namely, that
he had committed some offence, and was being
pursued by the police, and that not a moment
could be lost. The lady then desired him to
go into a closet, and locked the door on him;
which she had just time to do before the police
were heard in the house, having traced the man
into it. They insisted on searching every part,
which they did, until they came to the lady's
room, which also they entered, although she
was lying in bed, and apparently had just
awoke from sleep. They searched the room
thoroughly, tried the locked door, without sus-

pecting the trick, and then retired. When
the lady had dressed she released the prisoner,
and was so much interested by his story, that
she arranged for him to remain in that room
for a day or two, and pretending herself to be
ill—caused by the alarm—removed to another
room, where she had food brought, which she
divided with him, until the police, who were
stationed round the house for two or three
days, had withdrawn, when the man left,
overwhelming her with expressions of gratitude; and she never heard of him until two or
three years after, when a very gentlemanly-
looking man called to see and thank her for
her protection; which was to her the more
gratifying, as the offence committed was a
pardonable one. The story was told to Mr.
Smith, in the presence of others, by the lady
herself.

From Hill Place Mr. Smith removed his
hounds to Swanmere House, belonging to Mr.
Shearer; and here he lived most happily for

some time, until he was so unfortunate as to
lose his beloved wife. Her death was sudden,
and the supposed cause is one too mournful to
be dwelt on. Her funeral took place at Hambledon, in which church there are monuments
for several of her family. This sad event
made Swanmere distasteful to him, and he
therefore removed to Exton House, which had
been the residence of Mr. Wadham Wyndham.
Here his old friends kindly gathered around
him. One in particular was Mr. Nichol, the
Master of the New Forest hounds, whose character both as a sportsman and a gentleman
was such that there was no difficulty in getting pleasant parties to Exton to meet him.
His visits were usually on the Thursday, in
order to be ready for the Friday's meet.
Much useful information was gained from him,
for his science and experience were ever at the
service of his friends; and he was in every
way a most agreeable companion; not the less
so for mixing a touch of good-natured satire in

his discourse when he saw occasion. Though few men ever showed such good sport as he did with the New Forest hounds, he was but badly supported; and at last, in consequence of some captious objections, he resigned them. Shortly before he did so, one man rode over a hound called Gratitude, when Mr. Nichol shouted out, with a glance at the dissentients, who had been formerly his warmest admirers, "For God's sake, don't kill *Gratitude ;* it is already reduced to a hound's name."

They were pleasant parties at Exton ; where Sir William Hoste, Sir Francis Collier, Captain Olliver, and the Yorkes often accepted Mr. Smith's hospitality ; and he in return was most warmly welcomed by Sir Joseph Yorke and his lady (who was the Dowager Marchioness of Clanricarde) both at Sydney Lodge and in London. On one occasion they went together to see Miss O'Neill in the character of Belvidera, when Sir Joseph was so much affected at the distress of the heroine, that he

burst into tears, and left the theatre, saying
that he would go home and have his cry
out. Poor Sir Joseph, as is well known, was
drowned in Southampton Water, and at a spot
that was full in view from a summer-house
at Sydney Lodge where Mr. Smith had often
gone with him to view the sunset. A short
time after Sir Joseph's death, Mr. Smith
called on the family; and happening to meet
with the coachman, who was an old servant,
he heard from him a curious anecdote of the
deceased. It seemed that some time before,
Sir Joseph, when leaving for town, had given
the man directions to destroy a Newfound-
land dog, as it was old and almost blind.
The man did not like the commission, and de-
layed from day to day, until at last Sir Joseph
returned unexpectedly, and finding the dog
still alive, asked him rather angrily what he
meant by it. The man replied, that he had
not been able to make up his mind how to kill
him. The answer was, "Why, drown him, to

be sure; it's the easiest of all deaths, and the one that I should prefer for myself." If such was his wish, he had it.

Miss Urania Kington, who was the daughter of Lady Clanricarde by her second husband, was a constant rider with the Hambledon hounds; and she bore off the bell from most ladies that Mr. Smith ever met with, whether in the ball-room or when mounted on her favourite handsome horse Selim. She presented a silver hunting-horn to him, which he still retains, and which Lord Kintore so much admired that he sent for one exactly like it.

One of the pleasantest of the many merry meetings at Exton was when Captain Yorke, Eliot Yorke, and Henry Yorke, were present. "The mirth and fun grew fast and furious," sustained by Eliot Yorke's quaint and cheery sayings, and numerous songs by Captain Yorke, whose memory in that way was wonderful, whilst his never-failing good humour and cheerfulness were absolutely contagious.

Mr. Smith, as we have said, had early cultivated a habit of observation of the animals that he followed; and this enabled him not only to paint them, but to explain to others points in their habits that were "posers" to people who had not kept their eyes open as wide as he did. This soon became known; and accordingly he became a kind of oracle, often consulted, though very probably his advice was not always followed. Sir George Rose once called on him for the purpose of stating the following "case;" and his observation of the habits of the wild deer on Exmoor enabled him to reply satisfactorily. A party of gentlemen, having New Forest keepers and bloodhounds with them, chased an old stag until their horses would go no further, and only three of the hounds kept on the line. One of the keepers got a fresh horse, and went to look after them. He found the hounds lying down utterly exhausted a short distance from each other; and only a hundred yards off the fore-

most was the stag, lying down also; but on
the approach of the man, he rose quickly,
and went off steadily. The question was, was
the stag tired? Mr. Smith was able to reply
at once, "No; he had never gone at his
best pace, though the hounds did; he only
went sufficiently fast to distance them; and
such is the case with good old foxes." As a
proof of this, he related what he had witnessed
with one of the fleetest packs of fox-hounds,
being the one that Mr. Osbaldeston brought
with him to hunt the Hambledon country.
They started an old fox within fifty yards of
them, near Hog's Lodge, and they raced him
on the open down for a mile and a half, keeping him in sight, but never getting nearer;
nor did the fox mend his pace, which it was
afterwards evident enough he could have done,
had he thought it necessary. They ran on for
four or five miles more without one moment's
check, and then they came to another open
down, reaching a mile or so. Not one of the

hunters could now see the fox, and the hounds came to a sudden check on the middle of the down. Tom Sebright the huntsman, and Dick Burton the whipper-in, who were considered the two best men in the kingdom with hounds, tried all their craft; but the scent could not be recovered. Poor Sebright was quite aghast, and said to Mr. Smith, who was at his side during the whole run, " Well, I couldn't have thought that any fox could have run away from such a pack as this !" and he declared that he would write and tell his master of it; for stay in the country he would not. Getting a little calmer on the way home, he began to ask Mr. Smith if he could in any way account for their losing the fox. Mr. Smith replied, that the Squire had brought a picked pack of forty couple of hounds, not one of which was more than a four-year hunter. These hounds could race as fast as older hounds, if not faster; but had there been a few six or seven-year hunters among them,

these old hounds would have held the line and
not have gone beyond the scent; or perhaps
the check might have been caused by a flock
of sheep having been on the down before the
hounds got there. In conclusion, he suggested
that they might make a wider cast to the outside of the down; but Sebright, utterly out
of spirits, shook his head and went moodily
home. These hounds only killed seven foxes
during the fourteen weeks that they staid in
the Hambledon country, although Mr. Osbaldeston occasionally assisted in hunting them.
On these occasions, when a check occurred,
the pack was divided, and two casts made
right and left at the same time.

A simpler case than this New Forest one
was recently submitted to Mr. Smith by a
gentleman who has coverts in the Vine Hunt.
His keepers had assured him that when the
Vine hounds were running a fox through one
of his coverts, they saw the hunted one snatch
up a cock pheasant, and though they hallooed,

he did not drop the bird—was not that a very unusual thing? Mr. Smith replied, " No, not at all; keepers will say anything; but I would not believe it if I had seen it myself;" thus leaving his friend to form his own opinion.

After residing two years at Exton House, Mr. Smith resigned the Mastership of the Hambledon hounds, and was succeeded by Mr. John King, from Devonshire.

CHAPTER V.

Becomes Master of the Craven Hunt—A daring leap—The horse General—Repartee of Mr. Warde—Anecdote of H.R.H. the Duke of Gloucester—Troubles with young hounds—"A haunch of fox"—The Grey Wethers—The Swing riots—Gives up the Craven.

In the year 1828 the gentlemen of the Craven Hunt invited Mr. Smith to hunt that country, which offer he accepted. Some opposition came from Mr. Grantley Berkeley, who claimed the country as a relative of Lord Craven; but the club adhered to their resolution, and Mr. Berkeley withdrew. No time was lost in sending the Hambledon pack to the kennel at Hungerford, lately occupied by Mr. W. Wyndham, and before him by Mr. John Warde, the early "patron" of Mr. Smith. Mr. Smith's next step was to visit Mr. F. Villebois at Adbury, who kindly showed him the country; and at the meeting of the club a map was

produced, from which it appeared that several
of the coverts had been lent to adjoining
hunts—the Vine, Sir J. Cope's, Mr. Assheton
Smith's, and Mr. Moreton's (afterwards Lord
Ducie). It was resolved that the new Master
should claim these coverts, in order to show
that they belonged to the Craven country.
This was not a pleasant task; but Mr. Smith
acted on his instructions, and advertised these
coverts for the meets on the first week of
regular hunting. As he had expected, this
gave great offence to the Masters who had
hunted them before; and when it became
known that a fox was killed each day, he
received very angry letters on the subject.
He replied civilly to them all, stating that the
only object was to prove that they belonged
to the Craven country; and as that end had
now been answered, it was very probable that
they would not be hunted much, if at all;
only reserving the right to do so if required.
This satisfied all but Mr. Assheton Smith,

who hunted Southgrove, and he threatened loudly. It happened that this covert belonged to King's College, Cambridge, of which Mr. Smith's brother was a Fellow; and by his influence a notice was sent to the lord of Tedworth forbidding his hunting in it. After a while things and tempers cooled down, he was readmitted to Southgrove " on sufferance," and the two Tom Smiths became greater friends than ever.

During the ride that Mr. Smith took with Mr. Villebois to see the Craven country, they passed the wall of Elcot Park, which Mr. Villebois said was a great obstacle when hounds ran through the park. Mr. Smith pulled up, as if measuring the height, which was six feet two inches; and being seen to smile, he was told it was impossible for a horse to jump it, neither was it necessary, as there were doors in different places. He said nothing then, but bore it in mind. It happened, however, in the second year of his

H. DEL.   LONDON. CHAPMAN & HALL, 193, PICCADILLY, 1866.   DAY & SON LIMITED LITH

mastership that the fox led the hounds through
this park, and they followed through the holes
left at the bottom of the walls for game to
pass. The horsemen made for a door, but
found it locked. Mr. Smith, who was mounted
on the General, rode at the wall; but the horse
ran his head up to it and then stopped short.
He was then taken back about forty yards,
and again put at it, and being well spurred,
accompanied by a touch of the whip on the
shoulder, he sprang over, to the surprise, and
indeed horror, of the whole field, who thought
it an act of madness, as the rider does now.
On reaching the ground on the other side, the
horse's fore feet gave way, and he came down
on his chest, his rider's feet being dashed on
the ground in a way that gave an awful shock;
but the horse rose with him on his back, and
he kept his seat for a short time, but long
enough to allow him to stop the hounds. The
men in the mean time had forced the door:
when they reached him he was unconscious;

but they held him on his horse until he got home, when he was bled, and carried insensible to bed. In three weeks he was again in the saddle, when he was told by some of his friends that they had ridden through the door-way which he had cleared. This was certainly a most remarkable leap; but Mr. Smith is so far from being proud of it, that he never mentions it, and when others do, he condemns it as an act of wanton folly, which he would be sorry that any one should imitate. He rode the General for seventeen seasons, and then gave him to an old quiet coursing friend, who had him for five years, and then found him one morning dead in the stable.

In the first year of his Mastership of the Craven, where, as has been mentioned, Mr. Warde preceded him, Mr. Smith killed a fox which was so old that it had not a single tooth in its head. One of the Hunt met Mr. Warde shortly after at Hatchett's Hotel, and making a very solemn face, inquired, " Why, Warde, how is it you are not in mourning?" "What do you mean? who?" cried Warde, astonished. "One of your oldest friends," said the other, with a deep groan. "Who—who is it? tell me at once." "I will. Tom Smith has just killed a fox that you must have hunted a hundred times, for he hadn't a tooth in his head." "Oh!" said Warde, who was never at a loss for a reply, "that's my doing after all; I entered Tom as a puppy."

The Craven country is not a good scenting one, but it has always a good supply of foxes, and, notwithstanding park walls, is an easy one to cross. Still a fall can be had, if you desire it. It happened once that Lord Ailesbury had the Duke of Gloucester staying with him at Tottenham Park, and he invited Mr. Smith to come over to the shooting, and stay for the night. As he had a meet near that day, he could only accept the invitation to dinner; and knowing the covert where the shooting was to be, his dread was lest his hounds should be led towards it. As it happened, the fox did lead that way, and Mr. Smith felt obliged to keep close to the hounds, so that he might stop them if necessary. It was the end of October, and the ditches were full of grass; so he got two or three falls, one of them being in full view of the shooters, who had collected at one spot on hearing the hounds. The fox was killed in the open, and Mr. Smith was in time for dinner at Tottenham. He was seated nearly opposite the royal Duke, who addressed him with, "I hope you were not hurt when you had a fall to-day." His reply was, that he did not know which fall was alluded to. The Duke then said, "Pray, sir, if you have had several falls in one day, how many do you get in a whole season?" This appeared too absurd to need any reply, and he endeavoured to evade an answer by turning to his neighbour, when he was startled by the Duke saying, in a loud peremptory tone, " Sir, when I ask a question,

I expect an answer; let me ask you again, how many falls do you get in a season?" "Twenty, or more." "Twenty!" cried the Duke, and raising his eyes with a sort of devout expression, " thank God I'm not a fox-hunter!" which was followed by a roar of laughter from the company, Assheton Smith especially.

Mr. Smith again met his Royal Highness when he was shooting at Mr. Pearce's, of Chilton Lodge. Of course the Duke was placed where the best shooting was likely to be: he was constantly firing, and a fair number of head appeared on the ground at the finish. After the ladies had left the dining-room, the keeper was sent for to state the number of birds; and on Mr. Pearce remarking, "Why, that is six more pheasants than we had reckoned," the reply was, "Yes, sir; but we have since found six more that His Royal Highness shot at." To those who knew what an execrable shot he was, the "Aah!

I thought so," of the Duke was diverting enough.

During the summer time it was Mr. Smith's custom to visit as many celebrated kennels as he could, year after year, so as to mark the result of breeding from perfect or imperfect hounds, &c. He was, in the first year of his Craven mastership, thus engaged about a hundred miles from home, when he received a most unpleasant letter from the Marquis of Ailesbury, saying that the hounds had broken away from the men when at exercise in Tottenham Park, and had chased his deer; and unless Mr. Smith kept better servants, he could not allow the hounds on his property. Of course no time was lost in returning home, when he heard a sad chapter of accidents, though things might have been worse. Contrary to orders, his men had taken the young unentered hounds along with the older ones into the park for exercise, fancying that they were under good command. Unluckily a rabbit jumped up among the pack, and was pursued by the young hounds into some high fern, out of which leapt a fallow deer, after which they were in an instant. The men rode after them trying to stop them, but their hallooing and shouting had the contrary effect, by inducing the whole pack to join them; and then they were running full cry in various directions, and were only stopped when the herd of deer had got together in one corner of the park. It was fortunate that they did not lay hold of a deer; but it was with great difficulty that they were got out of the park, being kept at full gallop to prevent their turning back.

Mr. Smith took vigorous measures with the delinquents. On the day after his return he had a few of the wildest fitted with couples, to which was attached a piece of wood eighteen inches long; this threw them over on their backs if they attempted to run. Thus equipped they were taken towards the park, and when

within half a mile of it they appeared to smell
the deer, and made several attempts to rush
forward, uttering a frightful whine. They were
then severely corrected; after which they were
taken among the deer, when they became
quite furious, like mad hounds. Seeing this,
each hound was fastened to the park-pales,
and again flogged most soundly; after which
they were taken back to the kennel. Each
succeeding morning and afternoon saw a few
couples treated in the same way, until the
pack had been gone through; but it was not
thought safe to trust them until after cub-hunting, of which they had had none. On one occasion when they attempted to follow the deer
Mr. Smith had a narrow escape of his life.
He was riding in Savernake Forest adjoining
the park, and was going at a furious pace to
stop the hounds, when the dead branch of an
oak-tree pierced his hat, just grazing his head;
but he left his hat on the tree until he had
accomplished his purpose.

Before the regular hunting began, he had sufficient confidence in his hounds to fix the first day's meet at Tottenham Park. This brought together a large field, many of them reckoning on the death of a deer; but they were disappointed. Not one hound took the least notice of the deer, although on their mettle in chase, and they killed their fox. Before starting, one or two of the men had ironically requested a haunch of venison; and when the fox was killed Mr. Smith rode up to them, offering them "a haunch of fox," and telling them that it was only fair they should eat it.

It is only right to mention that when Lord Ailesbury heard of the reformatory measures going on, he kindly sent a live deer to be placed in the kennel, for the hounds to see and get used to, which had a good effect; and this was all the more kind, as his lordship had been informed by Mr. Assheton Smith that when once hounds had taken to deer they never could be broke of it. The object of this declaration might be to get the hunting of his lordship's extensive domain; but if so, the manœuvre failed, and the Marquis had no reason to repent his trust in the other Mr. Smith. The Craven hounds never again took notice of the deer, but worked so steadily that, though they had no cub-hunting that season, they killed ninety foxes in ninety-one days' hunting. It was luckily the best scenting season possible, and with scarcely any frost; but what with his exertions at starting, and his anxieties about the deer, giving him frightful dreams, the Master lost two stone in weight; which was better for his horses, if not for himself.

One day the hounds had killed a fox after a good run in Savernake Forest, and were about to return home, when Lady Elizabeth Bruce, the daughter of the Marquis of Ailesbury, who had been in at the death, rode back to say that the forest-keeper had just shown her a fox lying in the fork of an oak

tree at a great height from the ground, and
she was most desirous to see it hunted. Her
ladyship was one of the most fearless and elegant riders that ever followed hounds, and her
wish was law to the gallant Master. The
hounds were accordingly taken to the tree,
where the fox still was. A keeper ascended,
when the fox ran out to the extremity of a
large branch, and dropped from thence to the
ground, full forty feet. He ran briskly, apparently unhurt, and the hounds were laid on
the scent; but he saved himself by running
into Westwoods, where there were three other
foxes on foot.

It is not our intention to chronicle all the
good runs in the Craven country, but the
following one must be told, as it has a connection with a story to be related hereafter.
The meet was at Fifield, near Marlborough,
in consequence of Mr. J. Goodman having lost
a good deal of poultry, which was supposed to
be taken by a fox lying in Borum Wood; and

he would rather have lost the whole than have Reynard disposed of in any but a sportsman-like manner. On the arrival of the hounds at his house, he said to Mr. Smith: "You will laugh when I tell you something about my youngest boy. He is now at home for the Christmas holidays, and I had promised him a ride on his pony after the hounds to-day, if he first learnt his lesson in geography. I asked him just now the capital of some country, and his reply was, 'Borum Wood.'" By general consent the rest of the lesson was excused for that day, and the embryo sports-man accompanied the party to his "capital," where the fox was found, which after a good run in the open to the left of Marlborough, was run to ground under an immense stone, similar to those at Stonehenge. This was one of the Grey Wethers, which lie in a valley the south end of which terminates near the old Bath road, bordering on Salisbury Plain. It was impossible to get the fox out; but Mr.

Goodman was determined to prevent such an affair in future. He therefore sent fourteen of his strongest cart-horses, and men with tools, to move the stone; but without the slightest effect. Mr. Smith took great notice of this, and from his observation he formed a theory to account for the mode of building Stonehenge, which will be found in another chapter. Being able to do nothing more, Mr. Goodman had all the holes stopped up with stones, which it would seem that the fox found out. For when what every body thought was the same fox was found a few days after by the hounds, he broke away on the same line as before; but either from being pressed too hard, or from knowing what had been done, he returned to Borum Wood, and ran through that to Westwoods, an immense cover of several thousand acres. This had been anticipated by Mr. Smith, who was desirous to oblige so good a friend of fox-hunting as Mr. Goodman. Accordingly he had brought with him a larger pack than usual, ten couples of which were kept in reserve in an empty stable. After running for some hours in Westwoods, these fresh hounds were brought to the wood, and they soon killed the hunted fox. Strange to relate, his sides were of different colours: one was nearly black, the other the same as usual; so that during the run it was more than once thought that they were running two foxes. Major Hilliard begged the skin as a curiosity; and the poultry of Mrs. Goodman dwelt in safety for the future.

Mr. Smith being at Tattersall's one day, whilst he hunted the Craven, was introduced by Tattersall to Prince Esterhazy in terms absurdly laudatory, when the Prince told him that if he would go abroad, he should have the management of his pack of hounds; but he regarded the offer as a joke, though Tattersall assured him that it was in earnest. He never had any idea of residing abroad, and he soon after resigned the Craven. He sold his pack to

Mr. F. Villebois and Mr. Drax, the former of whom engaged to hunt the country. During his mastership of this hunt the " Swing" riots occurred, and a disorderly mob entered the town of Hungerford, where they regularly besieged the town-hall, in which the magistrates were assembled. Mr. Smith and other sporting gentlemen armed their servants and came into the town the next day, when the rioters sheered off; some of the ringleaders were afterwards hung at Reading.

Before quitting the Craven, mention should be made of Charles Treadwell, Mr. Smith's first whip, who was afterwards recommended by his master as huntsman to the Quorne, and also to the Bramham-moor Hunt, where his bold riding rather surprised them. On the above occasion, when Mr. Smith informed him that it had been resolved to meet the rioters, he instantly cried out, " Which horse shall I ride ?"

CHAPTER VI.

Second marriage—A theory on Stonehenge—Mr. Beckford's Letter on the Rights of Fox-hunters—Publishes "The Diary of a Huntsman"—A run with the royal stag-hounds—Death of Vampire—Plan for kennels and stabling.

WITHIN six months of his quitting the Craven, Mr. Smith married Miss Denison, of Ossington, the sister of the late Bishop of Salisbury and of Mr. Evelyn Denison, the Speaker of the House of Commons. Being shortly after on a visit to the Bishop, a party was made up to go to Stonehenge. On their return there was a discussion on that wonderful structure, in which Mr. Smith did not take part. This caused the Bishop to ask if he did not agree with the rest as to the almost superhuman character of the pile, and the inadequacy of any known means for raising it. He replied that he saw nothing so marvellous about it,

TO REPRESENT THE FORMATION OF STONEHENGE, ONE HALF OF THE MOUND OF THE GROUND
ALSO ONE STONE DROPPING INTO A HOLE AND TIPPING UP FROM THE PULLEY AND WITH A CONVEYANCE

LONDON. CHAPMAN & HALL, 193 PICCADILLY 1860.

DAY & SON LIMITED

TH. DEL.

and that he thought he could point out a way
in which it might have been constructed.
Pen, ink, and paper were forthwith placed before him, and he was desired to put his ideas
in a tangible shape. He at once made a
sketch (substantially the same as that on the
opposite plate), and the matter furnished conversation for the evening. The Bishop, looking at the sketch, allowed that there might be
something in the supposition, and next asked
where the huge stones at Stonehenge could
have come from. Mr. Smith then gave an account of a fox having been run to earth at the
Grey Wethers, and explained that those stones
are just of the same character; some of them
being twenty feet long, seven or eight wide,
and three or four thick. He allowed that it
would require a great number of men to trans-
port such stones for ten miles over Salisbury
Plain; but anyone who looks at the Wans-
dyke, which traverses the same district for
thirty or forty miles, will see that that is no

real objection. Whoever they were that dug
that wide dyke, and threw up that high bank,
must have had abundance of labour at command; and, though Mr. Goodman's fourteen
horses could not move one of the Grey Wethers, long levers very probably could. As Dr.
Johnson says in *Rasselas*, "the master of me-
chanics laughs at strength;" and Archimedes
had said long before him, "Give me a place
to stand on, and a lever, and I will move the
world."   Beside the explanation given by the
plate itself, it may be necessary to suggest that
trunks of oaks bound with iron, and pierced
with holes for levers, would furnish rollers to
propel the stones to very near their ultimate
destination.   It is also necessary to suppose
the site of Stonehenge occupied by a mound,
either natural or artificial; the ascent being
by an easy incline from the quarter whence the
stones were brought.   On the top of the
mound we must suppose as many holes dug as
there were upright stones to be placed. On

LONDON. CHAPMAN & HALL., 193, PICCADILLY, 1866.

DAY & SON, LIMITED, LITH.

HOW THE STONES OF STONEHENGE WERE PROBABLY RAISED.
IN THE VALLEY CALLED THE WITHERS.

the arrival of each stone, it would be dropped into its hole; and when all were thus placed, there would only remain the more easy task of laying on the imposts, each end of which evidently has been mortised on to the perpendiculars. The earth would then be dug away, leaving the structure complete; and if this earth must be accounted for, we may think it probable that we see it in the numerous barrows near, that still exist on Salisbury Plain.

Mr. Smith had the pleasure to meet Mrs. Ker Seymer at the Bishop's table. This lady was the daughter of Mr. Beckford, whose *Thoughts on Hunting* are so well known; and she kindly communicated to him the following unpublished manuscript of her father. As there does not appear to be any well-understood definition of the rights that constitute a fox-hunting country, it may be useful in avoiding or settling disputes, the writer being recognised as an authority wherever sport and sportsmen are to be found.

" You ask my opinion of the rights claimed
by fox-hunters; I will give it as concisely as
I can.

" Three distinct rights are to be considered
—*original, acquired,* and by *sufferance. Original* right undoubtedly belongs to the proprietors of the covers, &c. &c. where foxes
may be supposed to lie; but when once a pack
of fox-hounds is established in a country with
the consent of those proprietors, an *acquired
right* is then obtained, of which the said pack
cannot afterwards be deprived; unless, by an
uncommon misconduct on the part of those
concerned in the management of the hounds,
the proprietors themselves should think fit to
deprive them of it. This is the case of all the
old-established hunts in the kingdom.

" Right by *sufferance* is where a neighbouring pack avails itself of a vacancy; the
country at that time, by some accident or
other, being without any hounds. A blot is
no blot till it is hit, and this possession is

good no longer than it remains undisputed. Should the Duke of Rutland part with his fox-hounds, Sir Gilbert Heathcote may hunt the country; but should the Duke, or any other gentleman in that neighbourhood, claim the country with the consent of the proprietors, Sir Gilbert must return from whence he came.

"You ask if the purchase of a pack of hounds can establish a right? Most certainly not. The hounds are movable at the will of the purchaser, and may be carried into a distant country; consequently there can be no inherent right in them *when so removed*. When Mr. Blair disposed of his fox-hounds to Lord Craven, they were removed into Berkshire, and I took possession of the country.

"Covers must be regularly hunted to establish an exclusive right. Mr. Farquharson has bought Mr. Wyndham's hounds, and may hunt that country. But since the hounds have been removed into a distant and distinct country, in consequence of which *none* of the

Wiltshire covers will be regularly hunted, and
the greatest part of them not hunted at all,
should Mr. Wyndham, or any other gentleman
in that neighbourhood, at any time, think
proper to establish another pack (provided it
be with the consent and approbation of the
proprietors before mentioned), Mr. Farquharson
must resign the country.

" Should you ask *on what* these rights are
founded, I shall answer you in two words—*on
common sense.*

" Stapleton, Nov. 26, 1806."

Another visit paid was to Mr. Evelyn
Denison, at Ossington, who procured Mr.
Smith some sport with Lord Henry Bentinck's
hounds. The meet was in Lincolnshire,
twenty-eight miles from Ossington. One hack
and a hunter were sent on over night half-
way, and he rode another hack the next morning to the same place; the hunter having
been already sent on to the meet. He followed on the fresh hack, the other being left

for the return journey at night, which was
made very comfortably, after a good day's
sport. Lord Henry rode back some miles with
him, and gave him a message for their common brother-in-law, Mr. Denison, Lady Charlotte being Lord Henry's sister. It was, that
the young horse of his which he had sent for
the whipper-in to make a hunter of, was a
rank roarer; and what was extraordinary, this
was the ninth horse out of eleven that he had
sent that had become so; and the only way
that he could account for it was that they
were all very large horses. His lordship also
asked Mr. Smith whether he had ever heard
any cause for a horse becoming a roarer; who
replied that he had not: he never had but one
horse a roarer, and that was one of the largest
he ever possessed; indeed, he had scarcely
ever seen a small horse a roarer. The reason,
he thought, possibly might be, that as large
horses are the produce of a thorough-bred by
a half-bred, which produce may inherit part of

the shape or make of the one, and part of the
shape or make of the other, they may have a
small chest, though otherwise of large propor-
tions, and thus the lungs have no proper space
for action.

Whilst at Ossington Mr. Smith paid a visit
to Lord Manvers, who recommended him to
see the Duke of Portland's wonderful improvement of some poor land, commons, &c., which,
by irrigation, he had converted into valuable
pasture. His lordship was suffering from a
recent illness, and was not able to accompany
the party, although, owing to his florid com-
plexion, a gentleman remarked that he looked
very well in the face. With his usual ready
wit, his lordship replied, " I am very well *in
the face.*" The party returned much gratified
with what they had seen. Some time after
Mr. Smith accompanied the Earl to the meet
of Mr. Foljamb's hounds. The sport was very
indifferent; and, after losing their first fox,
they got tired of the funereal pace that seemed

to be in fashion; so they returned home, and occupied the rest of the day in inspecting the farm which his lordship held in hand.

After these visits, Mr. Smith and his wife settled down for a while in the cottage adjoining the lake in Bulstrode Park, which Mr. Florence Young, who was a connection by marriage, begged them to occupy, treating them with all possible hospitality and kindness. Here they were visited by Mr. and Lady Charlotte Denison during the Ascot week; the cottage, curiously enough, being one that Lady Charlotte's grandfather had built for his gardener. It is necessary to mention this visit, as it was the cause of Mr. Smith's first appearance as an author. He had long been in the habit of keeping a note-book, in which, when he returned from a hunt, he usually jotted down anything in relation to sporting that struck him as remarkable, and as not having been noticed before. Mr. Denison having perused these notes, strongly urged

I

their publication—which Mr. Smith would never have dreamt of—saying, "You ought to publish them, for they are really original remarks; a huntsman is rarely capable of writing, and thus whatever he has learnt dies with him." This seemed a sufficient reason for the venture; and accordingly the notes were digested in the course of the next six weeks, and published by Messrs. Whittakers, under the title of *The Diary of a Huntsman.* As everything in it was matter of fact, Mr. Smith was not surprised to find that it was well received; in a pecuniary point of view it was most successful; and but one sportsman ever endeavoured to criticise or contradict any part of it, stating that dew rose instead of falling, as believed by Mr. Smith.

Whilst residing at the cottage, Mr. Smith ventured once more to hunt with the royal stag-hounds, though this was not his intention when he left home; he only meant to see the stag turned out and then return. The meet was at Burnham Beeches; and after seeing the deer off, and the hounds had got out of sight, he was riding quietly on the turnpike road on his way home, when he was joined by the late Marquis of Worcester, who said directly, "I see that you despise this sort of hunting as much as I do;" his lordship also having left them. They trotted on until they came in sight of Maidenhead Bridge, and then, most unluckily, the stag and hounds crossed the road in front of them. The Marquis remained where he was; but Mr. Smith, wishing to see the hounds cross the Thames, rode hastily over the bridge and along a road parallel with the bank, when suddenly he saw the stag crossing. In a few minutes the hounds and all the field appeared, and all thought of going home was abandoned. He well knew that his horse had not had a gallop for the last month, as fox-hunting was over; but he thought that Davis and others who knew him would pronounce him "dead slow," or what not, if he did not go on; and he could not face that. So off he went with the hounds; and a most awful pace it was: he was determined to keep up with them, and he did it for several miles, until the stag ran through a doorway into a walled garden, when he quickly closed the door to prevent the hounds killing him. Here he and his horse remained for nearly an hour, until Davis and the field came up; but before that he saw that his horse was in a bad way, so he led him quietly to Twyford, and into a stable there, in which the poor beast had been but a few minutes, when he reared up, placed his forefeet on the manger, and dropped down dead. Thus, for want of a little self-control, he lost one of the best horses that man ever possessed, as will be evident from one or two specimens of his performances that we will now relate.

No horse ever passed him during the hardest run in the Craven country, or stopped him at any fence, though he could and did stop

others, including even a steeple-chase rider on
a first-rate horse. Jem Mason is alive, and
can vouch for the following statement. Mr.
Harvey Coombe's hounds found a fox at
Hodgemoor, and they ran to and through Mr.
Du Pre's park, straight to and over the high
oak-paling at the far end. Mr. Smith was the
first at the paling, mounted on this horse,
which carried him clean over. Jem Mason
only was near him, and was well mounted, but
he turned back; and then for several miles
across this difficult country no man · beside
Mr. Smith saw the hounds until they reached
a large covert. The next summer, when in
London, Mr. Smith went to Elmere's to look
at a horse, when Mason came up; and, in
answer to an inquiry whether he knew Mr.
Smith, replied, "Oh! don't I? why, he's the
only man that ever stopped me at a fence; he
did it at a rasper, Du Pre's park-pales, with
Coombe's hounds." Probably Anderson the
dealer heard of this, for he sent a groom

from London to Bulstrode with a cheque for
150 guineas to buy the horse; but his offer
was refused.

One Sunday, when returning from church,
Mr. Smith was surprised to see a carriage and
four drive up to the door. It contained Lord
Suffield and his brother-in-law Lord Gardner,
who, after apologising for coming on that day,
stated their object. It was to request him to
give his opinion on a plan furnished by a
London architect for a kennel for 100 couples
of hounds, and stabling for forty or fifty
horses, with lodging for men. The estimate
was 5,600*l.*; and they wished the work to be
begun as soon as possible, as Lord Suffield
had engaged to hunt the Quorndon country
the next season, and it was then the middle
of summer. On looking at the plan, Mr.
Smith at once saw that the architect was altogether wrong in his ideas, and also that the
whole thing could be done properly for one-
half of his estimate. This he explained to his

visitors; and, in consequence, they pressed him to return to London with them, which he did, in order to draw out a proper plan for the building. When this was done, on the following day, the architect was sent for, who approved of it, and offered to send his clerk of the works to superintend the building. Accordingly the whole party went down by rail the next day to the site, where Mr. Smith marked out the plan on the ground, and the foundations were at once begun. Lords Suffield and Gardner remained but a few days, which was all the better for the progress of the works, as they had several members of the hunt to dine with them at the hotel at Leicester, which caused late hours; and these never suited Mr. Smith, who had, beside, to see to the agreements with the different tradesmen—a matter that matched but badly with the joviality of a hunt dinner. He remained until he saw things so far advanced that there could be no mistake, and then left; but he returned when all was finished to see that all was as it should be, and that there were no over-charges. In consequence of this vigilance, the whole expense was but 2,600*l.* It certainly gave him a good deal of trouble, but it was a business of much interest to him; and he felt amply repaid when Lord Gardner sent him for his own use his peer's ticket for the Queen's coronation, which occurred in the next summer. He went early, and secured an excellent place next to the peeresses. Being so advantageously placed, he made some pencil-sketches of various parts of the grand ceremony, and returned home most highly gratified.

CHAPTER VII.

Declines the offer of various Hunts—Visit to Scotland—Residence in Dorsetshire—" Tremulous to her new Master."

DURING Mr. Smith's residence at Bulstrode he
received offers of various Hunts; but he did not
feel inclined to be confined to one place, and
so declined them all. Beside others of less
note, he had offers of the Bedfordshire, Hertfordshire, Sussex, Warwickshire, and the Vine.
In consequence of these offers he visited Lord
Tavistock at Oakley, and was, with Mrs. Smith,
often invited to Woburn. His lordship offered
to give him his hounds and eight hunters.
In the same way he visited Mr. Delmé Rat-
cliffe, at Hitchin, with whose hounds he was
much pleased; they had an excellent run, and
killed. With Mr. Calvert, who offered the
Hertfordshire country, he had capital shooting.

Mr. and Mrs. Smith paid a visit to Scotland, where they took a cottage at Kelso—the salmon-fishing in the Tweed being one great object; and Mr. Smith had good sport. They had acquaintances among the neighbouring gentry, and the time passed most agreeably. Field sports occupied the day, and the evenings were given up to dancing and singing, first at one friend's house, then at another. At Lord John Scott's they were most hospitably received, and at Sir Hugh Campbell's they attended a ball. First and foremost among their friends was Mr. Robertson, who kept fox-hounds at Coldstream, and had as huntsman Charles Treadwell, who had served in the Craven under Mr. Smith. Mr. Robertson is a "Liberal" in every sense of the word. He proved himself such in supporting the Liberal Governments of late years in all their wasteful schemes, such as for fortifications on Portsdown Hill, which would require half our army to man; and, in the better sense, of freely spending his own money also. For he had kept up entirely at his own cost a good pack of fox-hounds for several years, and had made many excellent gorse covers, well fenced in, on his property in Northumberland; and he is, beside, hospitable to a degree not often seen in the present day. Few men in the North will be so missed. His wife too is a most amiable and excellent lady, and her singing delighted her guests. In short, everything at Coldstream (Mr. Robertson's seat) was in keeping.

A curious incident connected with Mr. Robertson's pack must be related. After a very good run, the fox was followed into a large plantation of young firs, evidently beaten, and was viewed by Mr. Smith hardly able to go. At this moment the hounds changed to a fresh fox some distance off. Mr. Smith told Treadwell of this; but he only shook his head, and cheered the hounds away in the open. A single hound, however, stuck to the scent, and

in the course of a few minutes he was heard
apparently baying at an earth. Mr. Smith
rode up, and saw the fox, with his back close
to a furze-bush, fighting with the hound. He
got behind, and dropped the thong of his whip
close to the mouth of the fox, who bit at it:
this settled him, as Mr. Smith at once twisted
the lash round his mouth, and catching him
by the poll, carried him out of the cover. A
gentleman who was passing brought back
the pack, and they soon ate him.

Mr. Smith, whilst at Kelso, often hunted
with Lord Elcho's pack, which was a splendid
one, and he had some good sport with them.
The Duke of Buccleuch also had a clever pack,
though not so powerful as Lord Elcho's. Mr.
Smith hunted with them also, and found the
huntsman, Old Will, as Lord John Scott used
to call him, a fairish huntsman and excellent
servant, indeed far superior to what one often
meets with. Lord Elcho was a particularly
affable, agreeable man, a capital shot and fly-

fisher, and the best gentleman huntsmen that Mr. Smith had ever seen.

In returning from Scotland, Mr. and Mrs. Smith slept but one night at an inn, so many friends' houses were open to them; a very agreeable matter, although it made their journey rather slow. They visited, among others, Sir Mathew Ridley, when Mr. Smith had a day with his hounds (it was the last year that Sir Mathew kept them), and also painted a picture of her ladyship on horseback; she was a daughter of Lord Wensleydale, and a most charming person. After a short time they went into Dorsetshire, on visits to Lord Portman, Mr. Farquharson, and Mr. Drax. This latter gentleman had purchased half of the Craven pack, as already mentioned. At his splendid mansion of Charborough, Mr. Smith met Mr. Grantley Berkeley, who, it is hardly needful to say, was most excellent company. They then took a house for a few months at Bournemouth, and Mr. Smith amused himself with the shooting on Poole Heath. Whilst thus employed one day he moved a fox; and having informed Mr. Drax of it, the hounds were sent to find him, which they shortly did. They ran him across the turnpike-road, and to the left of it, straight to Christchurch Water, where they came to a check. John Last, the huntsman, gave him up for lost; but Mr. Smith told him that the fox must be gone back, and that if he trotted along the turnpike-road, he might probably cross the line of the fox where he had crossed it that morning. The place mentioned being full four miles off, this occasioned some surprise; but the advice was taken; and, on arriving at that spot, the hounds did hit off the scent as if close to him, and ran him to an earth near where he was first found, close to his brush.

After quitting Bournemouth, Mr. Smith resided for some time in a cottage near —— House, in Dorsetshire, the residence of a gentleman who kept a clever pack of hare-hounds.

This gentleman was an old acquaintance, and he was often supplied by Mr. Smith with small unentered hounds. Whilst Mr. Smith had the Craven, he had a most perfect very small bitch of his best blood, which he called "Tremulous." She had been entered, and made steady from hare and other riot, but was found too small for his pack. He therefore offered to give her to Mr. ——; but only on condition that he would keep her as long as she lived. This having been promised, she was sent, with the accompanying "copy of verses," to impress the promise on the gentleman's mind. Great was Mr. Smith's mortification when he heard, some time after, that it had failed to do so, and that poor "Tremulous" had been parted with, for three couples of hounds belonging to the Rev. J. R——, who kept a pack in Devonshire, and who was a first-rate judge of a hound.

TREMULOUS TO HER NEW MASTER.

" Craven-Hunt kennel, Hungerford.

" How oft in course of time we see
The fate of dogs and men agree !
How oft, as fate or whims incline,
Are both compell'd to change their line,
And slowly to retrace the road
With eager steps they lately trod !
    " Thus I, who once must never dare
E'en look at what is call'd a hare ;
With whom a rigid education
Had check'd each rebel inclination ;
Who never once was wildly bent
To revel in forbidden scent ;
And in preserves, through all temptation,
Had never stained her reputation,—
Must now forget each law and rule,
Each precept that she learnt at school,
And what she was condemned to hate
Pursue with ardour—such is fate !
    " Though this is dreadful innovation,
Yet Tremulous finds consolation ;
The comfort that she has, is knowing
The master's kind to whom she's going ;
For of that name some fame or word
Has surely reach'd to Hungerford.
E'en dogs have heard thy judging eye,
Thy huntsman's lore, thy merry cry ;
The triumphs that thy pack has had,
So oft by thee to victory led.
The wish express'd, late be thy end,
As husband, master, father, friend ;

Excuse my boldness, sir, for you're, we know,
Non magis Marti quam Mercurio.[*]
" When snow gives dull unwelcome rest
To hound and hare and scarlet vest,
And lake and brook, and hill and plain,
Are bound in Winter's icy chain,
Thou knowest, in thy well-stored mind,
Resource and comfort well to find.
Thy friends then, on the social night,
Hang on thy tongue with new delight :
When wit and learning take their turn,
They listen and or laugh or learn.
Full well by thee observed we see
The rite of hospitality ;
That sacred rite, whose gen'rous care
Angels ere now have deigned to share ;[†]
Perhaps, to bring thee nearer heaven,
It is to thee an angel given,
In whom th' admiring world may trace
An angel's mind, an angel's face.
And, oh! would Fate the bliss but give,
A bliss for which 'twere blest to live,
When trembling limbs and many an ache,
That dogs and men in age will shake,
And my last sand is nearly run,
Tell me my occupation's gone,—
Would Fate allow me to attend
That lady as a humble friend,
Sometimes to share the happiness
Of gentle word or kind caress,—
Then Tremulous indeed might say,
The dog has seen its happy day."

[*] Horace.　　　　[†] Genesis xix. 20.

K

Some time after Mr. Nichol gave up the
New Forest country, Mr. Smith was hunting
with the Forest hounds, when the following
incident occurred, which the Duke of Beaufort
(then Marquis of Worcester) may probably
recollect. The hounds had drawn one of the
large enclosures blank, and were about to try
some other covert, when his lordship told the
Master (who was also huntsman) that Smith
was certain that a fox was in it, as he had seen
two hounds, when wide of the pack, on a
strong drag of a fox. The pack was brought
back to where these hounds were seen, and
shortly found; and three other foxes were
viewed across the rides. It often happens that
coverts are not half drawn, in that country
especially.

CHAPTER VIII.

Becomes Master of the Pytchley Hunt—Management of the
hounds—Difficulties—Lord Spencer—Kind conduct of the
Duke of Buccleuch — Extraordinary runs — Resigns the
Pytchley—Hints on buying horses—An unpleasant adventure.

WHILST residing in Dorsetshire, Mr. Smith
received an invitation from Mr. G. Payne and
other members of the Pytchley Hunt to hunt
that country. Wishing to see all the best
hunting countries, he accepted the offer, though
he saw that he had an uphill task before him.
The Hunt had then no pack; but they proposed
to purchase that of Lord Chesterfield, who had
last hunted the country. This, however, they
failed in. Owing to his lordship's absence in
France, or some other reason, the pack was
not for sale until the end of October; and then
Lord Ducie outbid the Hunt, and carried them
off. He, however, only wanted twenty couples,

and he gave Derry, the former huntsman, all
the young unentered hounds to select them for
him. This being done, there remained fifty-
two couples for the new Master, to which he
added part of a pack from Wales; and with
these he had to commence on the 29th of
October.

On writing to the chief proprietors of the
coverts and lands within the Pytchley Hunt,
the new Master received replies from most of
them acceding to his request of permission to
hunt; but three or four stated that, unless the
establishment was conducted with more pro-
priety than had sometimes been the case here-
tofore, they would not consent; and one gentleman insisted on "Sabbath observance" on
the part of the men employed. Mr. Smith's
reply was, "that Sunday should not be dese-
crated by them, if he could prevent it," which
satisfied his pious correspondent.

In order to lose no time, he sent to head-
quarters the three horses that he already had,

and bought some more at the sale. The hounds
had physic; and as he wished to give them cub-
hunting in Sywell Wood on the next day, he
asked Lord Chesterfield's men—Derry, Goddard,
and Jones—to go with them; which they promised to do. But they changed their minds
in the course of the night; and when he went
to the kennel early in the morning, they told
him they could not go with the hounds, as
they were Lord Chesterfield's servants. This
was, in the language of diplomacy, "an unto-
ward event;" but the new Master had met
with and surmounted as great difficulties before, and he resolved to show the fellows that
he could do without them. He told old Hayes
the feeder, and Moody a helper in the stable
—who, as he knew, had occasionally ridden a
second horse—to get ready to go with the
hounds; and then went back to his lodgings,
where he put on his red coat, and filled his
pockets with bread and biscuit to throw to the
hounds on their way to the covert. As he

rode back, with his horn in his hand, he met
the malcontents, when Derry said, "I see you
are going to exercise them." "Oh! yes; I
hope they won't have too much of it." "Why,
surely you are not going to hunt them? you
can't know them, nor they you." "Never
mind—they'll know me as well as they know
you in an hour or two." This was received
with a loud laugh by the trio, as they knew
that the young hounds had never yet been out
with horses.

Having reached the kennel, he directed
Hayes, as soon as the hounds came out, to trot
off towards Sywell Wood (four miles off), and
not to pull up till he arrived there. Moody
was to bring up the rear, and the Master took
his place in the middle, speaking cheerily and
tossing biscuit to them. In this way they in
due time reached the field adjoining the covert,
when he halted them to recover their wind,
and dismounting, he walked about among
them. After half an hour or so spent in this

way, he threw them into cover; they soon found in the great wood, and they had very pretty amusement for an hour or two, when the fox took to ground, and the hounds were taken home. At the kennel the whole village was assembled, with Lord Chesterfield's men very busy in the crowd, foretelling that he would return by and by without the hounds, instead of which the whole fifty-two couples were with him.

After a day's rest the hounds were taken to Nobottle Wood, belonging to Lord Spencer, who formerly hunted that country. They soon found several foxes, and they ran one into a drain under a road in the wood. Whilst trying to get him out, Moody's horse having lost a shoe, he was sent to get another put on. Scarcely had he gone, when a view halloo was heard outside the wood, and the Master determined to give his pack a little more exercise. He therefore left Hayes to get the fox out, and though alone, took the hounds to the halloo.

They got on the scent, which happened to be
very good; and they ran their fox in the open
for nearly an hour, when they killed him.
Seeing two men on horseback in the wood, the
Master blew his horn repeatedly, until one of
them came up, who proved to be Lord Spencer's head-keeper. He began regretting that
"Mr. King" was not there to see the finish;
and, in answer to an inquiry as to who that
might be, he replied, "My lord's old huntsman, and the best that ever was." Just after
the hounds had eaten their fox, John King
rode up, got off his old gray horse, and walked
about wiping his forehead, and exclaiming,
"Well, this is wonderful!" for, of course, the
whole country well knew that this was an un-
tried pack, &c. Then addressing the Master,
he declared that he would write that very night
to Lord Spencer and inform him of all that
had happened. He was as good as his word;
for two days afterwards Mr. Smith had a most
friendly letter from Lord Spencer, saying that,

after what John King had said, he might rely
on receiving every assistance that it was in his
power to give. His lordship closed his letter
with a cordial invitation to Althorpe, of which
Mr. Smith subsequently often availed himself.
The days were given to shooting, and the evenings to cheerful conversation. His lordship
took great pleasure in speaking to his visitor
about the various public characters who had
borne a part in passing the Reform Bill; and
he had the portraits of many of them hung up
in his hall. After good John King had taken
his leave, the hounds were led home. The
way was mainly through pastures, where there
was no trace of a road; and old Hayes was
obliged to ride first to point out the way.
They had to pass through Brixworth, where
Derry and his two whippers-in lived. They
were standing at their door; and when they
saw the fox's head hanging from the saddle,
if they were pleased, they did not look so. On
the contrary, one bawled out savagely, " I'll

be —— if he hasn't killed an old fox!" The hounds were all got back safely, though, as the land near Althorpe swarmed with hares, there was some riot with the young hounds.

For the two following days the Master was busy with providing meal, hay, and corn for the cub-hunting kennel at Brigstock; and then he took all the horses and hounds there, and remained with them for a fortnight, in which time he killed nine foxes and ran several to ground. The country round belonged to the Duke of Buccleuch; his old and valuable head-keeper had orders to give every assistance, which he did, and there was an abundance of foxes.

Having thus blooded his hounds, Mr. Smith returned to Brixworth, and made known to Mr. G. Payne, Mr. Hungerford, and the others, that he could now venture to commence regular hunting; but that it was necessary for them to assist him in procuring a huntsman, as it was understood that he would

not hunt the hounds himself, and he had failed
to procure one by advertising. The first whip,
Goddard, on hearing of the sport that had been
had, had offered his services; and it was agreed
that he should be the huntsman, chiefly be-
cause he was a steeple-chase rider. Jones, the
second whip, and young George Turner, the
son of Lord Chesterfield's head-groom, were
also engaged. Goddard had hunted the hounds
six weeks, and killed only two foxes, when
Jones, the first whip, in defiance of orders,
persisted twice in a bad trick that he had of
riding to view the fox when in chase, though
not at check beyond any small covert. As
he was rarely in time, and if he was, he headed
a fox back, and was liable to halloo the hounds
on to a fresh one, he was told that if he did this
a third time he would be discharged. He then
did it more resolutely than before, and was dis-
missed that night. Within half an hour Goddard came in, and said that he thought Jones
had acted right, and as he was discharged, he

should leave also; which he at once did. And
it was no cause of regret; for he would never
have been fit for his post, as he took no real
interest in the sport. One day he had a good
run from Crick, but lost his fox. The next
day Mr. Smith was riding with him to cover,
and asked him how he had slept. His reply
was, "Very well—I'm very well." Mr. Smith
next asked, "Then what became of your fox
yesterday?" He replied, "I really don't
know—I have never thought of it since."
"What!" cried the Master; "find a fox, have
a good run, go to bed and sleep without thinking what became of your fox?—you'll never
be a huntsman as long as you live."

There was to be hunting next day; the
meet was to be at Crick, and one of the best
coverts in the kingdom was to be drawn there.
When the Master reached the town he found
there some hundred men in scarlet from all
the neighbouring hunts, and he had to ride by
them with Hayes and Moody in their shabby

old red coats; George Turner alone of his following being well dressed. He had prepared himself for all sorts of sarcasms, and so took no notice of the remarks that were freely made, as he felt sure that he could show them sport. Just before the throw off, Lord Cardigan inquired why the other two men were discharged. He received the short reply, "For disobedience of orders;" and, without asking anything more, said, "Quite right—but what do you mean to do?" "Find a fox, have a good run, and kill him." Turning to Lord Rosslyn, his lordship said, " That's plucky, isn't it?" and then introduced Mr. Smith, not knowing that they had already become acquainted in the New Forest.

The hounds were soon at work in that fine gorse of ten acres, having moved two foxes, one of which left the covert, and passed through a host of horses, thereby proving to the Master that he had some point; but no one else then thought so, for when the hounds ran to the

end of the second large field, where they threw
up, he heard such remarks as, "Here's a pretty
sort of huntsman." He told two men on foot
to get the fox out of a drain which he alone
had seen one hound mark, and directly led the
pack off to the far side of the gorse, rode into
it with them, and, as he expected, found the
other fox on the outside, ready for a start.
The fox broke away before any of the men had
got up, thus giving the hounds a better chance
than usual; and being well settled to their fox,
the men had quite enough to do to get sight
of them for at least a mile. On they went at a
racing pace for about half an hour, when they
came to a check in a road. The men were
now getting their second horses; and Lord
Cardigan, who regretted the check, was looking about for his, when Mr. Smith said to him,
"Never mind about your horse; the fox is
gone down the road, and we shall hit him off
before we get to the fresh manure-heap." They
then kept on together; the hounds hit off the

scent on the right-hand side of the road, ran for twenty-eight minutes across the finest grass country possible, and then ran into their fox. His lordship, who was the only man quite close to the Master, was much pleased and excited, exclaiming, "Capital! capital! *I'll* give you a character" (for Mr. Smith had mentioned his reply to Lord Rosslyn in the New Forest). The run lasted fifty-five minutes, and his lordship has often since said that it was the best that he ever saw; in fact, a better could not be, looking at the fine grass pace and time, and there being but one check.

Not long after this, the Master had supplied himself with proper whippers-in, but not with a huntsman, although he took every possible means to find one; whether his efforts were counteracted by any one, he cannot take on him to say. At the first meet after this they had another famous run, when, strange as it may sound, not one man besides himself ever saw the hounds after the first five mi-

nutes.   They found a fox in Yelvertoft gorse, a
small covert of four acres.   Though surrounded
by a large field of sportsmen (or at least horsemen), the fox broke through them, and was
apparently making for Hemplow Hills, where
are large coverts of gorse.   Just ahead was
an almost impracticable wide high hedgerow,
which the hounds shot through, and then were
lost to sight.   The Master rode over a single
high and strong rail and deep ditch, but was
not followed by one man.   After a chase of
several miles they killed their fox, but not one
else of the field was present.   It was only as
he was returning with the hounds that he was
overtaken by two of his men.   He was told
the next day by Mr. G. Payne that when the
riders arrived at the top of the hill, neither
horse nor hounds were to be seen, men went
galloping about in all directions, and the scene
beggared all description.

Shortly after the Yelvertoft run Mr. Smith
paid a visit to Mr. Vivian, in order to have a

day with the Bedfordshire hounds, of which
Mr. Magniac was then master. When they
reached the place of meeting, they found the
field waiting for the Duke of Bedford, who had
promised to be present. His grace on his
arrival inquired for Mr. Smith; and when he
came forward, told him that he had come pur-
posely to meet him, in order to ask him all the
particulars of that splendid run, and whether
it was true that he was the only man with the
hounds during the greater part of the run and
when they killed their fox. Having received
the required information, his grace left the field
without joining in the sport.

The Duke of Dorset was one of the chief
proprietors in the Brigstock part of the Pytchley country, and by his desire the hounds met
at Grafton Park (where was a large covert)
at three o'clock in the afternoon, as he had a
party of foreigners at his house, to whom he
wished to give some idea of English sport. In
the park is a circular space, with six roads

from it in the form of a star; three carriages containing the visitors were placed there, which gave them opportunities of seeing the foxes and the hounds crossing and recrossing, and afforded them great amusement for three hours, until the Duke thought it time to return home for dinner, but expressing his hope that the Master would bring an account of the day's sport. They killed soon after the departure of the Duke, and the brush was taken up to the house, when his Grace introduced Mr. Smith to some of the party, who were Italians, as "Il cacciatore di volpi." His Grace, as is well known, was one of the most finished gentlemen in the kingdom, and a most agreeable evening was passed. The strange exclamations of the foreigners had greatly amused everybody when in the field; but the amusement was quite as great afterwards to see with what surprise they listened to a few hunting anecdotes, and still more when told that the huntsman cheered each hound by name, and knew its tongue, when he heard it, even in the wood.

These two good runs, and his extraordinary good luck, led the Hunt to request Mr. Smith to continue Master and Huntsman also; and he went on with them for another season. Several other runs were remarkable enough; as one from Naseby to the Brigstock country; and another from Misterton, when he rode over the first brook that he had ever attempted; it was seventeen feet wide, and he had to cross it three times during the run. The only three men beside who rode at it failed; they were Mr. G. Payne, the Rev. Vere Isham, and Tom Goddard.

In the second season they met one day at Sulby, which was then occupied by the Duke of Montrose. Mr. Smith dined with the Duke the day before, and the conversation turned on an extraordinary run a few days before with the Quorn hounds, when the pack ran clean away from every horseman, owing to their having to cross a pasture of 100 acres, which was saturated with rain and very deep. Mr. Smith being asked what he thought of it, said he thought it a wonder that such things did not occur more frequently, as the hounds had no weight to carry. A hearty laugh was raised against him, and exclamations of "Why, such a thing had never been known before in that country," &c.; but he was able to bear it, for

> " A man convinced against his will
>   Is but an unbeliever still ;"

and though many years have since gone by, he has not changed his opinion. A distinguished party had assembled at Sulby, and he was able to give them a fine day's sport. He knew that a good fox would be found in Loatland Wood, which was nearly four miles distant; so he merely ran his pack through a covert or two on the way to it. When there, they immediately found; and their conduct impressed on him the belief that, from some cause or other, hounds might now and then be safely left to themselves during a run; for it so happened that only one man (Mr. Wheble, of Sir John Cope's Hunt) beside himself got clear over the wide brook; a few of the field got up with the pack before they reached Scotland Wood, where the fox was killed.

One more run must be related, as it was near the end of Mr. Smith's last season with the Pytchley Hunt. The hounds met at Fox Hall, a favourite meet, and shortly after found close by. They ran their fox for twenty-two minutes, over the finest turf, like a flash of lightning; after which they came to ploughed land and slow hunting, which allowed the fresh horses to come up. Although the hounds were still hunting, Sir H. Goodricke rode up to Mr. Smith, and told him that they all wished him to find a fresh fox. His reply was, "Certainly not;" adding, that the hounds would get up with their fox in Hope's plantation, just beyond. Sir Harry (who was Mr. Payne's brother-in-law) took back the message; but soon again rode up to say, that if he persevered, the men would all go home. " I can't help that," was the reply; "we can kill our fox without you." The Duke of Buccleuch, who was the only man that had kept close to the hounds, on hearing the last message, said that he thought at first that the gentleman was coming up to praise the hounds for working so well over the ploughed land, and expressed his hope that Mr. Smith would persevere. He did so; and on reaching Hope's plantation, a few minutes after, the hounds at once hit off the scent. Then they had about twenty-five minutes' racing pace over a fine grass country, and killed an old dog fox. His Grace, who was the only one there beside the Master, got off his horse, and requested to have the brush, although, as he said, it was the first that he ever took home in his life. He also said that that was the best day's sport he had ever seen, and that he would let the malcontents know what they had lost.

C DEL

L'SON CHAPMAN & HALL 193, PICCADILLY 1863.

DAY & SON LIMITED, LITH.

TWO OLD STAGS AT BOUGHTON HOUSE THE DUKE OF BUCCLEUGH'S
THE OLD ONE IN THE FOREGROUND WAS BRED IN SHAW ANTLERS

He expressed his regret, too, that Mr. Smith was about to resign the Pytchley, and urged him to come to Scotland to hunt with his hounds. His Grace rode twenty-eight miles to the meet the next day, for the purpose of telling the men what a run he had had; which he did, to their no small chagrin.

On one occasion the meet was at Boughton House, the seat of the Duke of Buccleuch, when, just before the throw-off, the keeper requested Mr. Smith to come with him to see a curious matter. It seemed that one of the watchers had that morning seen eight feet of deer sticking up out of the water; and when with assistance the two stags were got on shore, their horns were so tightly intertwined that it was impossible to part them. They were supposed to have been fighting, when one drove the other into the water, and was thus drawn in himself. They certainly presented a curious appearance as they lay dead on the grass. It is believed that the heads

and antlers thus locked together have been
preserved, as Mr. Smith suggested.

At the end of this, his second season, Mr.
Smith made known his intention to resign the
Pytchley country; and he carried it out, notwithstanding various letters of regret that he
received. One of these was signed by many
yeomen and farmers in the Hunt, and it stated
that the country had never been hunted more
satisfactorily even by the celebrated Mr. Mus-
ters or Mr. Osbaldeston. His twenty-two
horses were sold at Tattersall's; and they
fetched far more than merely remunerating
prices. This being a novelty when a Master
of hounds sends his stock to the hammer, Mr.
Smith has been asked to explain how it happened; how, in short, he had been able to
avoid purchasing at least some unsound horses.
The following is the whole of the mystery,
and he hopes it may be useful to some of his
readers.

His plan was, never to buy a horse without either riding it himself or having a written warranty. He made his choice of the two plans; and if it was refused, he never would buy. If the horse was at a dealer's in London, he commonly rode the horse in the Park, the dealer's groom accompanying him, trotted or galloped, and then took it back, saying that he would call the next morning. He did so, taking good care to make his call an early one, before there was time for any exercising; and if the appearance of the horse was then satisfactory, he closed the bargain.

On one occasion he was forced to make a trial of a horse's soundness in a more disagreeable manner. Owing to accidents with his horses whilst hunting the Craven, he was obliged to go to London to purchase a horse; and having heard of a likely one at Osborne's commission stables, he went there; and as he liked the appearance of the steed, and really wanted it at once, he ventured to buy it on a written warranty; but luckily he gave a cheque dated a few days forward. As he wanted to be back at Hungerford as soon as possible, he determined to ride the horse part of the way home, his groom being to come on by coach, and take charge of it the next day. He had ridden nearly to Staines, when he fell in with a mob of London roughs, who had come out to see a prize-fight, and having been baulked by the magistrates, were ripe for any kind of mischief. Two of these fellows were in a gig, whipping and galloping like mad; and when they came near him, though he had drawn up on the side of the road, they pulled the reins and attempted wantonly to drive over him. To save his leg, he struck at the horse's head to turn it away; but the blow caught one of the vagabonds on the nose, and covered his face with blood. They were in the act of jumping out to seize him, when he put spurs to his horse and galloped off. The whole rabble rout, horse, foot, and drags of every description, gave chase; and it looked

something very like a race for life. Finding
his pursuers gain on him, he rode at a fence,
but his horse fell at the ditch. The mob were
almost on him ere he could force his horse
over; and then many got into the field at a
gate near the spot, and chased him with cries
of "Stop thief!" and choicer exclamations.
Luckily the horse cleared the next hedge
and ditch, which some of the fellows rode at,
but only to fall head over heels. Mr. Smith
rode off, laughing at them floundering in the
mud, cleared the next fence into the road near
Staines, and stopped at the inn, to refresh both
himself and his horse. Soon after the ostler
came to say that the horse was very lame.
Mr. Smith went to the stable, and then sent
for a farrier, who proved to be a very respectable, intelligent man. They discussed the
matter over a bottle of port, when the farrier
pronounced the horse unsound, and pointed
out the marks of its having been lately blis-
tered on the lame leg. Mr. Smith sent the

horse back to Osborne, stopped the cheque at the bank, and heard no more of the matter.

This convinced him of the soundness of his plan of never purchasing a horse till the next day; and it also showed how much more valuable a man's own trial is than any warranty in the world. Indeed, he heartily wishes that all warranty of horses should be abolished by law, and purchasers be thus forced to exercise their own judgment.

CHAPTER IX.

Visits to Scotland, Yorkshire, &c.—Sir Tatton Sykes' establishment at Edlesthorpe—Anecdote of Sir Tatton—Castle Howard: runs with various packs—Anecdote of Lady Morgan—Visit to the Continent—Kindness of Mr. N. M. Rothschild and his family.

BEING once again out of harness, Mr. Smith occupied some considerable time in paying visits to various friends. His steps were first turned towards Scotland, where he was most kindly received by the Duke of Buccleuch, Lord and Lady John Scott, Lord Elcho, and others. Having taken his two horses with him, he joined the hounds whenever he had the opportunity, and saw some excellent sport with the Duke's hounds, as also with Lord Elcho's. Salmon and grouse were also duly attended to. The Duke, many years afterwards, writing to him at Droxford, assured

him. that he had not forgotten the best day's
sport that he ever saw in the Pytchley country
or anywhere else, and said that he had often
related the incident to others.

One of Mr. Smith's nieces married Mr.
Haigh, of Whitwell; and on her husband's
death, her uncle, being one of her trustees,
had annually to go into Yorkshire to see after
her affairs, and the management of her fine
estate, which lay in Sir Tatton Sykes' country.
He in consequence was invited to Edlesthorpe,
where the baronet at that time kept a pack of
fox-hounds, and he had good sport with them.
Sir Tatton also showed him over his establishment, which contained a numerous blood stock,
the produce of nearly a hundred thorough-
bred mares. Mr. Smith remarked that he had
never seen stock looking in such good condition, but of course they must consume an immense quantity of hay. His host replied that
they consumed no hay at all, as he would
prove to him next day. Accordingly he was

taken to see the mares, colts, and fillies fed,
when he found that their food entirely con-
sisted of oats in the straw cut into chaff; the
oats were cut before the straw was dead ripe,
and it was found to be almost as good as hay.
There were tanks kept filled with water, and
the whole of the stock was allowed to feed
without limitation. The plan seemed to him
well worth following by all breeders of horses
as well as by farmers. In each paddock there
was an excellent shed with long manger, and
about twenty colts or fillies were placed in
each. The viewing the establishment took
up two whole days, which were to Mr. Smith
the most interesting of the kind in his life.
He was also greatly pleased with a clever pack
of harriers which belonged to Sir Tatton's
young son (the present baronet), and which
he wished to cross with the blue mottled
Southern hound. Mr. Smith had a friend
who kept a pack of the old Southern hound,
and strongly advised the measure; indeed, he

thinks that even Masters of fox-hounds must shortly cross their high-bred hounds, and thereby regain noses.

In the dining-room there was a large picture, of which Sir Tatton told an anecdote in his peculiar quaint way. It represented his father and mother, with himself standing in front, dressed in a drab frock-coat, red waistcoat, and top-boots, and was the production of the best artist of the day. When it came home, there was, of course, a muster of the tenants to see it. All agreed that the likenesses of the old baronet and his lady were excellent, but, for some cause or other, the third figure seemed to puzzle them; probably the costume was not quite that which they were accustomed to see the young squire in. At last a light seemed to dawn on one of the party, and he cried out, "Oh! it's their old groom." Young Tatton was standing by, and said, with a polite bow, "Yes, it's their faithful servant, Tat," to the dire confusion of the honest farmer who had mistaken him for a groom. The story is not much in itself, but the mode of telling made it irresistibly comic.

Some time after this, when his niece had married again, Mr. Smith was invited to accompany her husband's brother, Mr. Stephens, to Castle Howard, where, by the united efforts of many guns, a heavy bag of game was got, which was forwarded to the Earl of Carlisle, who was then Lord Lieutenant of Ireland. This business being finished early, Mr. Smith, in compliance with a request from Mrs. Stephens, went into the picture-gallery, where were several paintings which she had most admirably copied. There he found an artist engaged in copying the Three Maries—a picture that he had often heard highly praised; and he asked how it was that one hand of our Saviour is painted fleshless, like that of a skeleton, whilst the other is full-sized and plump. The artist replied, " Sir, you have discovered the only fault in the picture."

M

Before quitting Castle Howard, Mr. Smith noticed on the first landing-place three landscapes painted with a great extent of sky. They are placed within the stone frames of three windows, and represent distant views. From the hall the deception is perfect; and the surprise is great when they are approached.

On another visit to Whitwell, Mr. Smith had a run with the York and Ainsty hounds, which were not generally considered to be good; but he found that it was not the hounds' fault. They soon found a fox in a large wood. The fox, after running a ring or two, with a good scent, through the open part, was lost among some large trees. Mr. Smith rode after the hounds; but the Master and others kept in a road in the wood, and called loudly to him that there was no way out in the direction that he was going. Yet, as the hounds did get out, he followed them, and had the pack entirely to himself. He did his best to assist them; and they were running fairly into their fox, which he had just viewed dead-beat before the hounds, when the huntsman and others galloped up, and, either from jealousy or want of sense, took the hounds in a contrary direction, made a cast to a large wood, and never got on the scent again. This is related to prove that where hounds go, a huntsman should go, if possible.

Among other visits, Mr. Smith paid one to Lord Spencer, at Althorpe, when he had a day with his old acquaintances of the Pytchley Hunt; Mr. G. Payne being now the Master. He was most cordially received; and when riding to draw the covert, Mr. Payne told him that they had been most unlucky, not having killed a fox for some weeks. As he was mounted on one of Lord Spencer's horses, and not on his own, he was obliged to decline assisting them, which he was pressed to do. They soon found; but after about half an hour's running they crossed the line of ano-

ther fox, on which the greater part of the
pack at once turned. He told Mr. Payne of
this; but as he had not himself noticed it, he
would not believe it, and merely said, "We
are all right."   Mr. Smith knew that they
were all wrong, and so he went on with the
few hounds that had kept to the hunted fox.
After running on capital terms for a mile or
so, he and these hounds viewed the fox, dead-
beat, run into a drain when only a few yards
from them. He was now at a loss; but luckily
a man on foot came up, whom he left to guard
the drain, whilst a mounted farmer kindly
rode after the hounds and brought them back.
Mr. Smith returned to Althorpe, as he did not
think it fair, when mounted on a friend's
horse, to attempt to catch hounds running.
He learnt the next day that the hounds were
brought back, and ate their fox.

When visiting his brother, the Rev. S.
Smith, at Weedon Lois, Mr. Smith hunted one
day with Lord Southampton's hounds.   After

a very good run into the Pytchley country the hounds came to a check, and the huntsman was about to give it up. Lord Southampton, knowing that Mr. Smith had hunted that country, asked him where he thought was the line of the fox. He pointed with his whip to the most likely line; and, on arriving there, the hounds hit off the scent, and ran a few miles further, still in the Pytchley country, when they came to what the huntsman pronounced to be a fatal check. Mr. Smith was again asked by his lordship to point out the line; which he did, indicating a large covert well known to him. When the hounds reached it, the huntsman looked so sulky, that his lordship pressed Mr. Smith to hunt the hounds for him. He declined this, but accompanied the poor fellow through the covert, where they shortly got on their hunted fox, and killed him after a few minutes in the open. Lord Southampton immediately jumped off his horse, snatched up the fox, and thrust it into the

huntsman's face, exclaiming, " Here's the fox
that you said was lost," &c. &c.

Not to make this work too long, we must
now mention but one more run, and that is of
recent date. The Hampshire hounds met at
Thedden Grange, and found in Southwood, in
the parish˳ of Shalden; a spot perfectly well
known to Mr. Smith, as the scene of his
boyhood. He viewed the fox that the hounds
had found, and at once told the Master (Mr.
Treadcroft) that it was a vixen (it was late in
the season); but the hounds were not stopped.
It ran straight for eight or nine miles to
Osden Common, which made the men laugh
and jeer at his taking it for a vixen; but the
result proved that he was right. When running through a large covert just beyond the
common, the great body of the hounds changed
to a fresh fox, and the Master wished to stop
the few that were going on with the hunted
one. Mr. Smith advised him not to do so, as
they were on their right scent; and the Master

rode off after the pack. Mr. Smith viewed
the hunted fox away from the covert, and followed the three and a half couple of hounds,
which killed it in the second field. He took
the fox on his horse, and overtook the pack at
a check, and threw it down to them. On
breaking up there were seen three very small
cubs.

Fox-hunting lore is not a very common
topic in a mixed company at a London dinner-
table; neither do ladies in general mix in such
if they should arise. But there are exceptions
to most rules; and so it fell to the lot of Mr.
Smith to be cross-questioned on the subject by
no less a celebrity than Lady Morgan. He
was dining at his sister's in Eaton-square, and
he had to take down her ladyship. During
the dessert some man opposite asked him if he
had a good entry of young hounds; to which
he replied that he had about fifty couple sent
out to walks. Lady Morgan at once brought
the conversation to a check by exclaiming,

"One hundred hounds!" and turning to Mr. Smith, said, "Will you allow me to ask you a question? Will you be so good as to inform me, after your experience, whether these hounds inherit most of their fathers' or their mothers' good qualities?" Seeing all eyes turned on them, Mr. Smith wished to change the subject, or at least defer it till they met in the drawing-room; but her little ladyship was not to be put off, so he met her question by another, Why she was so anxious to know this? She replied, that the fact was, she had studied human nature for many years, and the result of her observation and experience was, that all the most distinguished men then living were descended from clever mothers. She ran over a long list of names, including the Duke of Wellington, Sir Róbert Peel, Buonaparte, the Rothschilds, and many more, all of whom, according to her, had very wonderful mothers indeed. How much longer her list would have been it is impossible to say, had not the hostess risen to leave the table. On meeting again in the drawing-room, Mr. Smith was at once assailed for his "experience;" and he got rid of his questioner as quickly as he could by saying that the great object in breeding hounds was to supply any defect in either father or mother by crossing with another that had not that defect, but that, contrary to her ladyship's theory, young hounds inherited the qualities of the father rather than of the mother.

Probably it was Lady Morgan's modesty that hindered her from enumerating any of her own sex as indebted to clever mothers, or she might very fairly have quoted Madame Montefiore, the sister of the late Mr. Rothschild, who was certainly one of the most clever and accomplished ladies that Mr. Smith has ever known. She was the intimate friend of himself and his wife, and they visited her both in England and abroad. She had a house near Cuckfield; and hearing that they were about to pass that way on a journey, she pressed them to stop there for a day or two, although she was not able to be present to receive them. They went, and found that every possible attention had been ordered to be paid, which was most fully carried out, and the only drawback was the absence of their kind friend. They passed a Sunday there; and not knowing whether there was a pew attached to the house, they were rather at a loss; but they found an agreeable occupation in reading some beautiful Jewish prayers, a book of which was placed in every room. They were very much gratified with their visit. They were intimate with other members of the Rothschild family; and the present Baron Lionel took Mr. Smith into the country to see his pack of staghounds. The visitor was much pleased with the clever pack and all the appointments, and he expressed his regret that they were not in Devonshire to hunt the wild stag; they would, he said, fly over any bank, &c. "No doubt," replied the Baron, "there are plenty of banks in that country, but we have a much better one in London." "And which," said Mr. Smith, "will never give you a fall."

The friendship of the Rothschilds was of great service to Mr. and Mrs. Smith when they made a tour on the Continent. Furnished with a letter of introduction from the head of the house to his brothers at Frankfort, &c. they met with every possible courtesy from those gentlemen; and they found the name of "Rothschild" as potent as that of an emperor in removing the various difficulties that then beset the untravelled English. The letter was as follows:

"Gentlemen, I have the pleasure of introducing to you Thomas Smith, Esq., a very respectable gentleman, friend of mine, who is travelling with his lady for pleasure. You will receive them, both him and his lady, in the kindest manner; render them every assistance in your power, and contribute by

your civilities and attentions to make their
journey agreeable to them.   Offering my anti-
cipations, I remain, brothers, yours truly, N.
M. Rothschild."

It need not be said that the gentlemen thus
addressed most fully carried out the recommendation it contained.   Such, of course, was
to be expected; but it was really ludicrous
to see the effect that it produced on other
bankers in Germany.   At first they absolutely refused to receive the English money
which the party tendered; but the very name
"Rothschild" opened their eyes on the instant,
and they became even troublesomely forward
in offering accommodation of every imaginable
kind.   They went, with their brother-in-law,
Mr. Marx, in the Batavier to Rotterdam; and
then proceeded to Frankfort, where M. Rothschild put his box at the opera at their disposal, and gave them an English dinner of roast
beef, &c. every day, saying truly that they
would not see much of that when they got

further into Germany; and, knowing that Mr.
Smith was a sportsman, offered him the range
of his extensive forests; but unfortunately his
guest was not able to avail himself of this.
Thence they proceeded up the Rhine, halting
at all the remarkable points, and so into Swit-
zerland, where they stayed several days at
Berne, and still longer at Geneva, on a visit
to Madame Montefiore, at her villa in the
Campana Diodati.

CHAPTER X.

Returns to England, and resumes the Mastership of the Hambledon hounds—Purchases the Fir Hill estate, Droxford—His " Good-bye Day."

ON his return to England, Mr. Smith was much urged by the gentlemen of the Hambledon Hunt to take the Mastership again. It was not his wish to undertake so troublesome a task; but as no one else seemed likely to do it, he agreed to act for a single year, on the express condition that they would provide a proper successor in that time. He then rented Fir Hill, Droxford, where he erected a temporary kennel, and Mr. Long gave him two lodging-houses for the hounds. These houses formed a great inducement to him, and he would not have undertaken the Mastership without them; but when the time came for removing them, they seemed likely to be more plague than profit. It appeared quite impossible to the builder of them to remove them to Droxford, which was four miles off, and the way lay through narrow cross roads, so he absolutely refused to attempt it; so Mr. Smith undertook the task himself, and he succeeded. The houses did not receive the least injury, and they were the source of much wonder and amusement on their journey.

Finding no one come forward to take the hounds at the expiration of the year, Mr. Smith bought the estate of Fir Hill, and took to the pack in earnest. He went on with them for some years, having several very good runs and tolerably fair sport all through. In the last year of his Mastership twenty-nine and a half braces of foxes were killed, hunting three days a week. His last meet, which he held on a bye-day, and styled a "Good-bye Day," was deemed worthy of special record in the *Sporting Review*, and is reprinted here, by the permission of its author (Colonel, now Lieut.-gen. Elers Napier).

"GRAND FINISH" OF THOMAS SMITH, ESQ.

AND

THE LAST DAY OF THE SEASON WITH THE HAMBLEDON HOUNDS.

" The Hambledon hounds will meet on Monday at Horndean Gate ; Wednesday, at Shidfield ; Friday, at Corhampton Down ; Saturday (A 'GOOD-BYE DAY'), at Broadhalfpenny Down, at a quarter before eleven."—*From the Hampshire Chronicle of March* 27, 1852.

"WHAT the deuce have we here?" said I, placing the newspaper, in which I had just read the above announcement, on the breakfast-table before me.

" Saturday," continued I, in a half soliloquy, and half addressing an old friend who happened to be staying with me at the time ; " Saturday was generally a 'bye day' with the Hambledon—but then it was never advertised ; besides, I think that my friend Smith is taking a good deal upon himself, thus to foretell that it will be a 'good' bye day. Suppose, after all, it should prove a blank; what a laugh there will be at his expense!"

"No," continued I, smoothing down my chin (we didn't then wear beards,‧ more's the pity)—"no, Tom Smith—or 'Gentleman' Smith, as he is most appropriately often called—is too old a bird to expose himself to be pelted with 'chaff;' depend upon it, there is more in this paragraph than 'is dreamt of in our philosophy;'" and I forthwith handed the mysterious document to my companion.

"You may be a philosopher," said Staveley, with a most provokingly intelligent smile, "but, old fellow, you have most assuredly proved yourself no conjuror; it is evident that this is a little *jeu de mots*, implying that it is to be likewise a 'good-bye' or farewell day. But although, of course, aware of his being a 'mighty hunter,' I had no idea that your friend Tom Smith was such a wit as to be capable of perpetrating this atrocious pun!"

"Tom Smith," replied I, "is capable of

N

anything; he is an author, an artist, an architect; he is, in fact, everything, but more particularly—as all the world knows—a first-rate
sportsman, and a capital fellow to boot."

"And have you long known this incom-
parable mortal?" inquired my companion.

"Yes, many years; and our acquaintance
commenced in rather a curious manner, which
I will tell you, if you feel inclined to listen to
a 'yarn.'"

Staveley expressed himself desirous of hearing my story; which I commenced as follows,
in the old " story-telling" strain:

"Many years ago, I used to hunt with the
Hambledon hounds; I was in those days
younger, and rode rather wilder than I now
do in my old age. Well, I had then a most
remarkable mare—I called her ' Very Lively'
—and lively enough, in all conscience, she
was. No day was too long for her, and no
jump too high, provided she was allowed to
take it in her own way—always at a fly;

never had she made a mistake, and never till
the day I became acquainted with Tom Smith
had she ever felt the touch of either whip or
spur.

" On that day the hounds—on good terms
with their fox—were going across a close
country at a slapping pace. 'Very Lively,'
jostled by an awkward fellow at a weak point
in a stiff fence, made her first *faux pas*— it
was certainly only 'a very little one,' as said
Captain Marryatt's lady's-maid; however, to
recover her, I had to lift her with both bit
and spur. This indignity her proud spirit
could not brook; she threw up her head, took
the bit between her teeth, and for a time was
beyond all management and control.

" There was but one practicable outlet to
the field, across which she was flying at the
very top of her speed—and that was a stiff
five-barred gate, over and under which the
whole pack was streaming as I approached.
All my efforts to turn or stop were of no

avail. I saw, on nearing the gate, that I had only a single remaining chance. I gave her her head; I gave her, at the same time, both whip and spur. She shot past the foremost horseman, who had just pulled up—and then like a rocket shot over the gate, taking also the whole pack at a single stride—with three hounds struggling at the time over the topmost bar — and without touching a single hair !

"By the time I had succeeded in somewhat pacifying my irate and fiery steed, the quondam 'foremost horseman' was by my side.

" 'It is not often, sir,' observed he, 'that I like to see a man go before me over a gate; but I should have been very sorry to have been before you just now !'

" Well, this was my first acquaintance with Tom Smith; and I should like much to see this his last 'good-bye day,' if such indeed it is meant to be. What say you? Are you game for a gallop with the Hambledon hounds next Saturday from Broadhalfpenny Down ?"

Staveley readily entered into my plan. Our arrangements were soon made, and at the appointed day we found ourselves punctually at the meet. A glorious sun—quite a " soleil d'Austerlitz"—shone brilliantly on the numerous field then assembled at Broadhalfpenny Down. Men came from far and near, to witness the last " finish" of their veteran sportsman chief—to hear the last " whoop" of the man who had so often afforded them recreation, health, and sport—who had so often been the means of baulking their doctors of the accustomed fee! We mustered about a hundred and fifty strong, in scarlet and black and green. All the "beauty and fashion" of Hambledon—no contemptible display of both —were on the ground; and several ladies, appropriately equipped for the chase—amongst whom shone the fair " Huntress of South Hants" — came likewise to participate in

the toils and pleasures of the expected
sport.

Many a long day had passed since I had
had a turn with my old Hambledonian friends;
and so engaged was I in greeting a host of
well-remembered faces, that I had little leisure
to bestow for scrutinising the present establishment of the "Hambledon hounds." I,
however, missed an acquaintance of "auld
lang syne"—Squires, and also the second whip
of former days. Champion, the present head
whip, had all the appearance of being of the
proper sort: light, wiry, active-made, and
was said to be a first-rate rider. The hounds
—about twenty couple—struck me as rather
small, but seemed to be well matched, and
in capital condition. The horses of the establishment showed work; and though they
proved up to the mark, yet what can be expected on a subscription little exceeding 600*l.*
a year, wherewith to keep forty-five couple of
hounds, nine horses, and two whips?

Whatever man can do, Tom Smith has
done; and that he has given general satisfac-
tion who could deny, on witnessing his last
brilliant farewell field? That he has met
with one or two cavillers, is no less true; for
how difficult is it to please "all the world and
his wife to boot!" and what saith the poet on
the opinion of the multitude is most correct:

> " He that depends
> Upon your favours swims with fins of lead,
> And hews down oaks with rushes. Hang ye! Trust ye?
> With every minute you do change a mind ;
> And call him noble that was now your hate—
> Him vile, that was your garland."

Too often in the hunting-field do we find
this precept applicable to a few, with whom
one unfavourable season will efface the recol-
lections of previous unrivalled sport. The
veteran's proud spirit could ill brook the cavils
even of those few, who may have had some
imaginary cause of discontent; wherefore he
resigned the onerous post he had been solicited
to occupy—which he had so ably filled: and

I shall now endeavour briefly to describe the glorious finale—the last splendid run, afforded to a most select and numerous field, by the late Master of the Hambledon hounds, on this his last concluding day.

*   *   *   *   *

A more appropriate locality could not have possibly been selected than Broadhalfpenny Down: the spot fixed for the "rendezvous" of the large field, assembled on the 3d of April 1852 to witness the performances of Tom Smith's closing reign; in a most wild and picturesque-looking valley, embosomed amidst the green turfy slopes of the downs, partially clad with venerable woods, brown heather, or glistening under the influence of the golden and perfumed furze:

> "Delightful scene!
> Where all around was gay—men, horses, dogs;
> And in each smiling countenance appeared
> Fresh blooming health and universal joy."

Time is up! The "Master" arrives, and

mounts a powerful, sporting-looking chestnut
mare. Now,

> " Huntsman, lead on !   Behind, the clustering pack,
> Submiss attend, hear with respect thy whip
> Loud-clanging, and thy harsher voice obey."

Whatever may have been Somerville's,
such, however, is not Tom Smith's style of
leading his hounds to the covert side.   All
was done most quietly, and as a matter of
course, till his fine manly and deep-toned voice
was heard arousing the echoes of Highden
Wood. He appeared to me to draw hastily
through this extensive covert, from whence, in
times gone by, I had seen many a good fox
unkennelled, and had enjoyed many an ex-
hilarating run.   Highden proved blank; with
the same unaccountable and apparently care-
less haste did we next try Tiglace Gorse and
Wood.

I could not help remarking on this appa-
rent remissness to an old *habitué* of the hunt
—a remissness so completely at variance with

what I remembered of Tom Smith's usual persevering and unremitted endeavours to find his fox.

"Have a little patience," said the gentleman whom I addressed; "I'll be bound for it he has some object in view, and knows right well what he is about. I shouldn't wonder if he has an eye to Stoke Down, and to the fox there, which beat him a short time ago."

My friend's prognostications proved correct; and to Stoke Down Gorse we now trotted rapidly away. Here I recognised at once Tom Smith of former days. Amidst an apparently boundless extent of stiff unyielding furze immediately dashed in the huntsman and his whips. All their efforts were, however, long of no avail: there was, apparently, not even the slightest appearance of a drag—nothing, under the withering influence to scent, of a hot sun and dry easterly wind, to encourage the gallant pack in breasting the formidable thorny *chevaux de frize* impeding their onward progress through the stunted and prickly gorse.

Nearly an hour had elapsed; not a challenge had been given, not a tongue was thrown; all—save when some complaining hound got entangled amidst the labyrinth of furze—all continued within the dense thorny covert, silent as the grave. The forenoon was passing rapidly away, the heat of the sun was becoming momentarily more great, thereby, of course, decreasing our chances of a run, even should we be successful in a find; and although the hounds were mute, a few croakers began already to give tongue, and the face, or rather faces, of the field became overclouded with disappointment and " hope deferred."

Not so our gallant and persevering chief, spite of continued failures—whatever might have been his reasons—he seemed convinced that Stoke Down Gorse contained a fox; a gallant one, and one destined to give him a last splendid run.

The unfortunate "whips," whose legs had
been martyrised by wading so long through
this ocean of unyielding thorns, had just remounted their nags, after pulling off their
boots in order to clear them of the prickly
furze with which they were filled; the hounds,
with drooping, blood-tipped sterns, sneaked
out, all looking most unhappy and abashed.
I concluded we had—after, as I thought,
every possible effort—again drawn blank, and
that we were now about elsewhere to try our
luck.

Such, however, was not the case. Trotting
back along the edge of the "fretful" and much
"fretted" gorse, Tom Smith still persevered,
and, like a skilful general looking out for some
weak point in the enemy's stronghold, appeared determined to make one effort more
to dislodge him from his place of strength.
I happened to be close behind him at the
moment when I observed him to check his
horse, as "Destiny," a favourite bitch, sud-

denly threw up her nose and appeared to sniff the "tainted" breeze—but tainted only, as a less experienced observer might have imagined, with the powerful aroma of the flowery gorse—for not even a whisper responded to that whiff—

> " Or in triumphant melody confest
> The titillating joy."

Far otherwise, however, thought the veteran chief, who intently watched and followed his "Destiny's" unerring steps. The hound evidently feathered on the drag, and was eagerly cheered on into the furzy brake by Smith, who rode into the very midst of it himself. Then next occurred an anxious moment of suspense.

"Destiny" now threw her tongue; "Barrister" and "Barmaid" instantly responded to the joyful sound. The fox had evidently been moved. Tom Smith eagerly exclaimed, "By Jove! here must be a fox, for I see the furze quivering not two yards from my horse's feet."

"I'll bet a thousand pounds we've found him," added he, as he cheered in the now assembled pack.

A find indeed it was, and a more beautiful one a sportsman could never wish to see. We were near one extremity of the gorse, around which, in every direction, was scattered the numerous field I have described. What if, after all this trial of patience, crowned finally with success, our fox should unfortunately be chopped, and our anticipated sport nipped in the very bud? With less skilful management, such a contingency might probably have occurred; but Tom Smith, having shown how by sheer perseverance he could find his fox, now showed how—having found him— he would insure us a gallant run.

Not a moment was to be lost; the obedient pack he kept so well in hand, that they followed at his horse's heels, as the latter bored through, or sprung over the opposing furze, on which the rider now perseveringly plied his heavy whip. I shortly observed, immediately in his front, a tremulous movement midst the summits of the blossoming gorse— an universal opening cry next proclaimed sly Reynard to be a-foot. Tom Smith had fairly whipped him up, unkennelled him from his snug warm berth; he broke gallantly through his surrounding foes, full in view away, with every hound well laid on, and a hundred and fifty horsemen thundering in his rear. Straight down wind he went; then led us at racing speed for upwards of a mile, along the magnificent, smooth, and turfy slope of Stoke's undulating Down.

The pace was too good to last; so probably thought friend Reynard, who, even during this short but rapid spurt, drew after him a "tail" fully as long as that of Dan, the great Hibernian fox of old. Turning, therefore, sharply to the left, he next—cutting the turf—tried the fallows and high lands. Here, under a blazing sun, with a dry easterly wind sweeping over a hard parched-up soil, he probably flattered himself that he could give us all the slip. He had, however, reckoned without his host; for Tom Smith was of another mind. The scent, it is true, was often lost, but as often hit off again by most masterly forward casts.

In vain did sly Reynard try every artful dodge. The turf he liked not, the fallows would not do. The hounds stuck to him in covert, through Wallop, Stoke, and Brookes' Woods. He tried to ring it back to Stoke Down Gorse; and next—apparently as a last resource—seemed to make for Waltham Chase, taking in his way Soberton race-course Down.

His previous circuitous flight, together with a check or two which had recently occurred, enabled the greater part of the field to come up, as the hounds hit him well off again, on the northern side of the race-course, when a scene took place such as is seldom recorded in the annals of the chase.

From the Droxford and Hambledon road,
the race-course—a beautiful piece of turf—
slopes down for about a mile into the hollow, where lies imbedded the rural little
village of Soberton. Over this smooth vel-
vety slope the hounds now rattled along at
their topmost speed, closely followed by the
whole field *en masse*, and having more the
appearance of a furious charge of cavalry
than aught else I can describe. Thus they
thundered along in the "race of death" which
was shortly to ensue; for our fox—which
proved *not* to be a vixen, as some of the
"knowing ones" had predicted—after a chase
of fifty minutes, at a clipping pace, was run
into and killed in an open field, close to the
southern extremity of Soberton race-course,
where this splendid "charge" had taken place.

Never, perhaps, was there a more brilliant
finale to the reign of any Master of hounds.

The steady perseverance manifested in
drawing for his fox; the thorough scientific

knowledge of his craft, and of the habits of that animal, so clearly evinced by the nature of the "find;" the self-possession and coolness he had so opportunely shown in preventing him from being chopped when first on foot; his numerous and judicious casts when there appeared not to be a particle of scent; the successful manner in which he had contended throughout the day with what to some would have proved the most baffling difficulties, and managed to keep his pack on the very best of terms with their quarry,—all tend to show that the author of the *Diary of a Huntsman* and of the *Life of a Fox* could in an exquisite degree combine practice with theory in that most difficult science of the chase; a pursuit followed by so many, but in which are found so few proficients, such as the late Master of the Hambledon Hounds has ever proved himself to be; and on this occasion all agreed that he had fairly surpassed himself.

A hundred voices were loud in their con-
gratulations, a hundred hands pressed forward
to grasp that of the veteran leader of the
chase, a hundred applications were, in most
cases vainly, made for some relic of the fox,
to preserve as a memento of so memorable
a day.

In the midst of all his triumph, the " chief"
forgot not the dictates of that gallantry for
which he had ever been so famed; he had
promised the "last brush" to one of the two
young ladies who were present at the end of
the run. But the fair " Huntress of South
Hants"—fair in every sense of the word, and
one of the most graceful, accomplished, and
dashing horsewomen I ever beheld—protest-
ing that she had not fairly won it, most
courteously, and amidst murmurs of applause,
handed the much-envied trophy to her sister
Amazon of the chase, whom she averred had
been in before her at the death.

Thus smiled on by beauty, and amidst the

unanimous plaudits of this numerous and brilliant field, was sounded the "whoop" of "Thomas Smith, Esq., late Master of the Hambledon Hounds."

CHAPTER XI.

Publishes "The Life of a Fox, written by himself"—Visits the Duke of Beaufort at Badminton, and Lord Fitz-hardinge—The bull-dogs and the bear.

ABOUT 150 of the members and residents of the Hambledon Hunt joined in presenting Mr. Smith with a piece of plate, on his retirement.

Being once again his own master, he took the opportunity of hunting with various packs of hounds far and near, and enjoyed much excellent sport, though he could not help thinking that a mistake was now and then made even by very clever huntsmen. This occasioned him to compile a small work on hunting, which he styled *The Life of a Fox, written by Himself*. It is illustrated from his own drawings; and one plate represents a gathering of foxes from various hunting countries that had been visited by the writer, where each fox relates by what mistakes of the huntsman he had saved his life. The justice of the strictures was acknowledged by many Masters of hounds; and some of them even thanked the author for having thus cured their huntsmen of faults which they had not been able to correct. The autobiography of "Wiley," the hero, is made the vehicle of conveying a good deal of information on the habits of the fox, which shows the writer to be a man of acute observation.

Among visits that Mr. Smith paid were several to the Duke of Beaufort and Lord Fitzhardinge, which deserve mention.

At Badminton he spent a week, and hunted with the Duke's hounds. Long, the huntsman, told the Duke that only two or three couples of the hounds could feel the scent; which seemed to be the case, as they had then hunted five days without killing. His Grace asked Mr. Smith to speak with Long about it in his presence. Accordingly he said to him, "If two or three can hunt a low scent, why not have a whole pack to do so?" "But how can such a pack be got?" said Long. Mr. Smith replied, "By breeding only from hounds that can hunt a cold scent; you'll then often have a fair day's sport, when other packs can do nothing; and in a short time you'll have beauty as well as nose." The Duke then proposed to cross with the blood-hound, but was told by his visitor that it would not answer. He himself had crossed with Lord Ailesbury's famed bloodhound Wisdom; and even the third cross did not do. Although they had nose and deeper tongue, they never tried to be at head during a run, and they followed over at fences, so that they would be ridden over; in fact, they had not the dash of the fox-hound. This was an opinion that he had long before expressed to Lord Fitzhardinge, who quite agreed with him.

Mr. Smith had two or three good runs with the Berkeley pack; and he was much better

pleased with them than with the two bull-dogs
in the dining-room, from which he once had a
very narrow escape. His lordship one morning
took his gun to shoot wild geese; but as one
man has a better chance than two if together,
his visitor preferred to spend the morning in
the stable and the kennel. He was crossing
the moat on his way to the garden, when he
suddenly heard and saw the two bull-dogs
rushing straight at him. He instantly threw
his red pocket-handkerchief to a distance,
clapped his hands, and hallooed them towards
it. The noise was fortunately heard by the
old butler, who called off the brutes, and prevented their doing further mischief than tear-
ing up the handkerchief instead of its owner.
When his lordship was told of this, he shook
his head, and said, "You have had a narrow
escape;" which indeed seemed to be the case,
judging from instances that he mentioned of
the ferocity of these dogs. Why he kept such
savages about him as he represented them to

be, it is hard to say; for though he was notoriously fond of practical jokes, this seemed carrying that sort of thing rather too far. But the very next day he played off another joke. He and his visitor, on their way to the stables, passed a hutch in which a large bear was lying, confined by a chain; and he called Mr. Smith's attention to it, getting him to come quite close. Then he quietly loosened a large heavy block, which lay on higher ground, and it rolled down on the bear, which, being struck on the paws, growled furiously, and darted out to the extreme length of its chain, to the amazement, if not terror, of one of the party. Yet, in spite of these drawbacks, the visit to Berkeley Castle was a most agreeable one, and Mr. Smith was frequently afterwards invited.

As may be guessed from the expression of Mr. Smith, that "he had reduced falling to a science," it was at the cost of many a broken bone that he gained that knowledge;

but the most severe accident that ever befell
him was not in the hunting-field, but at the
Botley railway station. He arrived there one
evening from London, and it being very dark,
he did not perceive that the train had stopped
before reaching the platform. On stepping
out, he fell, his shoulders coming heavily on
the further rails, and he was taken up sense-
less. Recovering a little, he was laid on the
floor of the carriage, and conveyed to Bishop's
Waltham, when he insisted on being placed
in his rough pony-carriage and taken home,
knowing from experience that the motion
would prevent the blood congealing. The
doctor thought that both his collar-bones were
broken; and so they were, but that had been
in hunting years before. This accident confined him to the house for three months.

One remarkable accident occurred to him
in his seventy-fifth year, which may be noticed here, although it is not the last that has
befallen him. The hounds were running a

fox, a few couple only leading, when they went over the fence into the enclosure at Wickham Lodge. Nearly all the field went on to the gate, but one man stayed with him; and they both went over the fence together. Unluckily one horse fell, and threw his rider close before Mr. Smith. He, to avoid him, pulled his horse on one side, and so came in contact with a branch of an oak-tree, which caught him in the chest, and knocked him backwards over the tail of his steed. He fell heavily on his head and shoulders, and suffered great pain; but he mounted his horse, and joined the other men. They urged him strongly to go home, but he told them that this was contrary to his practice; and he remained with them to the end of the day. However, he could not hunt again for several weeks; which was no wonder, as a distinguished steeple-chase rider out that day stated that this was one of the most dangerous of falls.

For this and for other wonderful escapes Mr. Smith sincerely trusts that he may never close his eyes at night without returning his humble thanks to the Almighty, who has so mercifully preserved him, enabling him to exceed the allotted age of man, without having to say, "Few and evil have been the days of my pilgrimage."

As to gun accidents, which sportsmen so frequently suffer from, Mr. Smith has had several narrow escapes; but he never met with any other damage than the charge of small-shot which he received when a boy. One narrow escape was when shooting with Mr. Campbell Wyndham in Bottom Coppice. He happened to be placed near a noble lord; and whilst they were chatting in a low tone, his lordship's piece went off, and the charge passed over his companion's shoulder. His lordship, not at all disconcerted, shouted out, "Mark, cock!" and put his finger to his lips; thus enjoining secrecy on his companion.

Though Mr. Smith knew that the "accident" was the result of mere carelessness, he comforted himself with the idea that it might have been worse, as happened to Lord Eversley at Basing Park. Mr. Smith was invited to be of the party; but he did not arrive till the second day, when he found that his lordship had left, having been accidentally shot in the eye by one of his fellow sportsmen. Mr. Smith wrote to condole with his lordship; and in a few days received a note from him, in which he said that he was recovering from the accident, but added, "They did not tell you the best part of the story, which was, that, after I had been shot myself, I brought down the bird shot at!"

The next day he saw a young sportsman in a plantation of high firs, who was kneeling on one knee, intently waiting to knock over any hare or rabbit, and quite forgetting that he was within shot of a gun on each side. Mr. Smith roused him by asking whether he also wished to be shot in the eye, in preference to receiving the charge on his thick leather leggings.

A nearly fatal accident occurred quite recently to another friend, and which is mentioned here as a warning to those who delight in novelties. Last August Mr. Smith received a haunch of venison from Lord Gage, and a day or two after came a letter, dated from Firle Park, in which his lordship said: "I, directly after shooting the deer, wished to try the merits of the new gun-cloth ammunition; and I shot at a water-lily in my water three times with it, each shot of which dropped in the water short of the mark aimed at, although I rested my gun against the tree to steady the aim. I then took my son's gun to fire the fourth charge, when it burst at the breech, and both locks were driven away; one of which passed close to my son's head, and the stock was blown to atoms; one part passed over my shoulder, and tore off a large piece of the bark of the tree."

CHAPTER XII.

Life at Fir Hill—Serves the office of High Sheriff of Hants—
Various suggestions and improvements.

HAVING finally retired from the mastership
of hounds, Mr. Smith naturally expected to be
allowed to withdraw himself altogether from
public life. Not that he desired to live idly,
as the following pages will show, being quite
prepared to fulfil all the ordinary duties of a
country gentleman; but he was disappointed.
The higher powers called on him to serve the
office of High Sheriff of his native county of
Hants for the year 1858; and he entered with
all his accustomed energy on this new field of
duty. On his very first attendance at the
courts at Winchester he was forcibly struck
by the amount of crime that seemed indis-

putably traceable to the utter want of decent
sleeping accommodation among the cottagers;
and the practical result of his exertions was
the formation of a society for building additional bedrooms to cottages, so that no cottage
should have less than three; which has already
done much good in his district, and well de-
serves to be imitated in others. A plan of the
least expensive of these cottages is given.

On the same occasion, whilst as High
Sheriff he was awaiting the arrival of the
Judges at the railway station, two recruiting
parties came in, which, as he learned on inquiry, had obtained only two recruits in six
weeks; and on being asked the reason, they
replied that "the people didn't like soldiering
now." This Mr. Smith mentioned to the
magistrates, when spending the evening with
him, according to custom, and he suggested
that the boys in parish-schools should be
taught the rudiments of drill by the police, as
likely to give them a taste for the army. The

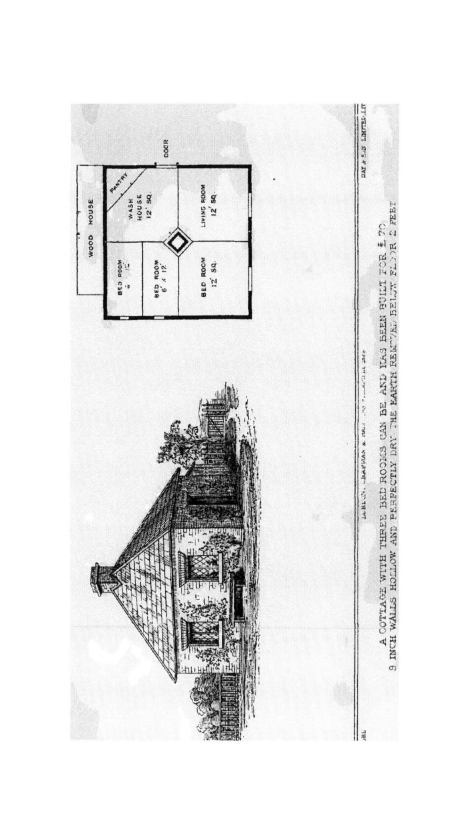

A COTTAGE WITH THREE BED ROOMS CAN BE AND HAS BEEN BUILT FOR £ 70.
9 INCH WALLS HOLLOW AND PERFECTLY DRY THE EARTH REMOVED BELOW FLOOR 2 FEET

WOOD HOUSE

PANTRY

WASH HOUSE 12' SQ.

LIVING ROOM 12' SQ.

BED ROOM

BED ROOM 6' x 12'

BED ROOM 12' SQ.

DOOR

DAY & SON, LIMITED, LITH.

Duke of Cambridge heard of this from some one; and Mr. Smith shortly after received an official letter from the Horse Guards, thanking him for the suggestion, which, as it said, H.R.H. the Commander-in-Chief considered the most valuable and practical suggestion that had been offered on the subject of recruiting for the last half century.

Shortly before the time that the Volunteer movement was begun, but when uneasiness had been already created by the swaggering speeches of the French Colonels, Mr. Smith was present at a dinner given at Alresford to the Master of the Hampshire Hounds, and the company paid him the usual compliment of drinking his health as an old Master. In returning thanks he recommended the gentlemen and farmers of the Hunt (about 150 were present) to practise rifle-shooting, so that they might be prepared to form a mounted troop of fox-hunters. The matter was a good deal talked of; and the result was the formation, some six months after, of the now well-known First Hants Light Horse, or, it is more commonly called, the Droxford troop; Colonel Bower, to whom the great success of the corps is justly to be attributed, being a resident in that village, and his efforts being efficiently seconded by Mr. Charles Sartoris, of Warnford Park. Mr. Smith holds the post of guide in this corps; and though he served in his father's company nearly sixty years before, he has shown that he is an " efficient member," and so earns the Government grant; for on a comparatively recent occasion he hit the target at 900 yards with the short rifle of the corps, and afterwards hit the target twenty times following, scoring 32 points. Proof positive of good eye and good nerve at 75! The late Lord Herbert of Lea, who had often hunted in the Craven when Mr. Smith was Master, took great interest in this mounted corps, and he wrote to his friend, promising to visit him at Droxford on his way home after the session of Parliament, in order to witness

its system and drill. Illness, however, prevented this, and he went abroad for the winter.
He returned to England in the following July,
and wrote to Mr. Smith from Dover, saying
that the state of his health rendered it impossible for him to visit Droxford. This must be
one of the very last letters written by this
most amiable nobleman, as it bears date but
three days before his death; and it is hardly
necessary to say that the relic is most carefully
preserved.

It has been stated that in early days Mr.
Smith was destined for the military profession;
and though he was obliged to adopt another
line in life, he has ever retained a lively interest in matters connected with "the pride,
pomp, and circumstance of glorious war." The
account of the doings of the Confederate ram
Merrimac, and the Monitor, led him to turn his
attention to the use of iron in warfare; and the
practical result was the construction of the
model of a locomotive battery to travel on

common roads. It consists of a cupola, constructed of iron, armed with one heavy gun, but large enough to hold, beside the gunners, ten riflemen armed with breech-loaders. He sent the model to Lord Palmerston at Broadlands, who passed it on, with the expression of his high approbation, to the War Office. Then it was examined in the Ordnance Department; and Mr. Smith soon after had a letter, stating that the battery was a most decided novelty, but that circumstances did not call for its adoption at present. The model was afterwards, by Her Majesty's command, taken to Osborne for her inspection, and it has since been exhibited in the Hampshire Loan Collection at Southampton in August 1866, where it excited much attention. The reader will gain some idea of what the locomotive battery is like from the accompanying sketch. Its size is proposed to be 12ft. high, 18ft. wide, 18ft. long, which would allow it to move along any ordinary road by means of Boydell's endless

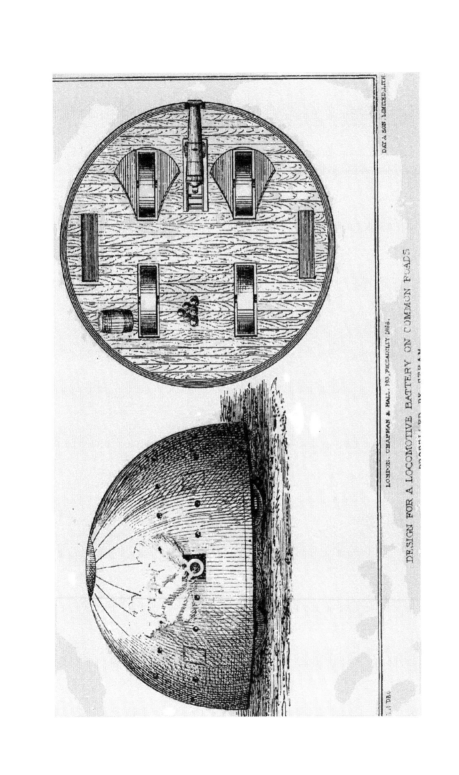

DAY & SON, LIMITED, LITH.

LONDON, CHAPMAN & HALL, 193, PICCADILLY, 1855.

DESIGN FOR A LOCOMOTIVE BATTERY ON COMMON ROADS

railway. Such batteries being stationed near
the coast might easily be placed in threes, so
as to command every road threatened with invasion, and again shifted, if necessary, to follow
the motions of the enemy.

It may here be mentioned that in the same
Exhibition were two spirited pictures by Mr.
Smith; one being a sporting piece, representing
the stag at bay in the New Forest, already
alluded to, and the other a scene of villagers
preparing for the marriage of the clergyman's
daughter next day.

A visit that Mr. Smith paid to Ryde, where
an invalid relative of his was resident, led him
to devise the tramway on the pier that has
since been carried out, and adds so much to
the comfort and convenience of all who resort
there. He sent the plan to Captain Brigstock,
an active director of the Pier Company, who
soon wrote to say that it was highly approved
of, and would be carried out forthwith; but
that the feeling among the porters, piermen,

&c. was such that if the projector appeared on the pier, he would stand a chance of being thrown over. This feeling, if it ever existed, has long died away, as the tramway has been found as advantageous to these men as it is to the public, enabling them to earn a better living, and with less labour, than formerly.

Mr. Smith having in early life given much attention to agriculture, and having always retained his interest in the subject, was led to think that the sewage matter of towns might be turned to good account in place of the imported guano, the stock of which bids fair to be soon exhausted. Accordingly he prepared a plan for so dealing with the sewage of London, which he submitted to the Speaker, at the time that a committee was sitting on the subject of the purification of the Thames. The Speaker in return sent him a number of official reports on the subject of the application of the sewage of towns, and expressed his concurrence in his views. His plan was very like

MINIATURE COPY OF THE FIRST PLAN FOR EMBANKING THE THAMES.

LONDON. CHAPMAN & HALL, 193, PICCADILLY. 1866.

DAY & SON LIMITED, LITH.

what has since been adopted. He proposed to have a drain 30 feet wide between the Thames and the houses on its bank; to intercept the sewage, and convey it to a few miles from London, where it might be prepared as manure and sold; also to replace the present shabby waterside premises by handsome buildings, with a broad road in front, having a stone wall to keep out the river, and with space also for a railway, if desired; in short, as may be seen from the accompanying plan, a foreshadowing of the Thames embankment and railway at present in progress.

When, some years since, it was proposed to make a sunken road through Hyde Park, Mr. Smith sent a suggestion to Lord Carlisle, the Chief Commissioner of Woods and Forests, on the subject. His proposal was, that the earth excavated should be deposited in the Serpentine by means of a movable tramway, and be spread over the bottom; thus reducing the depth of water to four and a half feet, and

so removing all fear of fatal accidents from im-
mersion during frosts, by which the expense
of the Royal Humane Society's receiving-
houses, icemen, medical attendance, &c. would
be saved, and yet sufficient depth of water left
for summer-bathers and pleasure-boats. And
if the road should not be made, earth for the
above purpose could readily be found by removing small mounds, thus levelling the park,
and improving its general appearance.

Waltham Chase, which is in the neighbourhood of Mr. Smith's residence, was enclosed a
few years ago, when allotments were made to
the cottagers; but they were not able to turn
them to much account for want of a plough.
Mr. Smith saw at the Colchester Agricultural
Show a newly introduced one-horse plough,
which seemed to him just suited to their circumstances. It was made by Ransom, of
Ipswich, and was called the Buffalo. He
bought one, which he tried on his own land,
where it was drawn by his old white cob,

thirty-five years old, and it ploughed an acre a day. He then lent it to the cottagers, where it did equally well. He sent an account of its performances to Ransom, who afterwards informed him, that in consequence of his letter being published, he had sold upwards of 2000 of these ploughs in eighteen months.

The renovation of worn-out pastures is a matter that Mr. Smith has pursued with great success. His plan is as follows. A turf three inches thick is turned over by a plough, to the hinder part of which two iron tires are attached, which break up the hard ground at the bottom of the furrow to the depth of four inches: a man follows, who drops in suitable manure. When the pasture has been thus gone over, the tires are removed, and the plough replaces the turf. Rolling shortly removes all trace of the plough, and the improvement of the pasture is remarkable.

Mr. Smith's garden at Droxford is surrounded by nearly all the trees in the village; consequently the birds hardly allowed a single bunch of currants or any other fruit to ripen. To keep off these marauders he has devised the following plan, which is not only effectual in saving the fruit from being devoured, but also allows him to have it in perfect condition much longer than his neighbours; the currants, for instance, generally remain nearly till Christmas. He built a wall ten feet high, with southern aspect, against which cherry-trees are trained. At the foot of the wall are strawberries. Then come, trained on wire, gooseberries, currants, and raspberries in rows, with narrow paths between. Iron rods placed here and there serve to support a sloping roof, front, and sides of galvanised iron wire netting, three quarters of an inch mesh; and the whole is secured with a door and lock and key. The " safe," as it may be termed, is 60 feet by 10 feet; and the cost of the whole was under 10*l.*

Two inventions by Mr. Smith, which must

be of especial interest to sportsmen, remain to be noticed, viz. clipping horses, and the "Iron-Duke" bit.

In the year 1814 he had an old chestnut hunter, whose coat was so long, that after a day's hunting it was almost impossible to get it dry till the next day. He therefore desired his groom to cut off the long hair from the underpart of the body; but the effect was so frightful, that, directly he saw it, he seized another pair of scissors and assisted the groom in clipping the horse all over; not having the use of a comb, of course it was notched dreadfully. A few days after this he rode the horse to meet the Hampshire hounds at Brookwood, causing great amusement, especially when Foster, the huntsman, exclaimed, "Why, Mr. Smith, the rats have been eating your horse's hair off." He replied, "Never mind; he'll go the faster for it," which was verified, for he certainly did; and Admiral Halkett bought him for eighty-five guineas. This becoming known to Lord Robert Grosvenor, he had his old black hunter properly clipped, which before was supposed to be worn-out by age; in consequence, as his lordship was often heard to say, of the clipping, he afterwards carried his rider as well as when he was young. This brought the system into fashion; and certainly every groom ought to touch his hat to Mr. Smith, as it is a wonderful saving of labour, and allows one man to do three horses in the time he would have to give to two, beside the clipped horses looking so much better.

The well-named "Iron-Duke" bit enables light weights effectually to control the most spirited horse without injuring it; and it may well be called also the "safety bit" for ladies and children, as no horse will pull against it. Like others of Mr. Smith's inventions, it was devised off-hand, to meet a present emergency. He had a desperately vicious horse, which ran away with him on Broadhalfpenny Down.

Finding that he had no control over the beast, he leant forward, when he at once discovered the cause, namely, that his tongue protruded, so that it formed a cushion, and thus prevented the bit resting on the sides of his mouth. The horse ran straight to and over the fence of Highdown Wood, until it was stopped by a high ash stem. Mr. Smith then dismounted, tore off the strings of his waistcoat, and tied the bit under the tongue. When they got again on the down, the horse started off, but was instantly stopped without the slightest difficulty, though he groaned with rage at being thus beaten; and from that time a lady or child could stop him, even when with hounds. Mr. Smith gave the proper directions for making the bit to Mr. Lachford, and it very soon came into use. Among other gentlemen, Sir Henry Peyton tried it; and so highly did he approve of it, that he ordered it for all his twelve horses, both for riding and driving, and he told the maker that it was the best bit he had ever seen, and that his letter might be published.

The following is an extract from a letter to Mr. Smith from Mr. Miles, who wrote that clever work, *On the Horse's Foot:* "It has long been an object with me to get a bit which will give me perfect control of my horse without inflicting torture on the poor beast; and that I have accomplished in your bits. The number and variety of bits now by me which I have tried bear ample testimony to the sincerity of my wish; and I shall certainly continue to make use of your bit both for riding and driving, and shall advise all my friends to do the same," &c.

This gentleman was a perfect stranger to Mr. Smith; and it may be right to remark that the latter has no interest in the bit, except the hope and belief it may be useful.

The foregoing are but a sample of various suggestions and improvements that have had their rise in the quiet of a Hampshire village. More might be added; but probably these will suffice to show that Thomas Smith of Droxford has done some good in his generation.

POSTSCRIPT.

MR. SMITH's recipe, after a fall with hounds, was put to the test on Saturday, November 24th last. During a good run with the Hambledon hounds, and when within three miles of the finish, his horse swerved directly after a leap, and carried his rider against the branches of a large tree, which struck him on the face, and knocked him backwards, clean over the horse's tail. He was stunned, and felt great pain, but insisted on being helped on his to get at a cottage close by. Lulling his pain, he rode after and overtook the hounds within three miles; and the fox was actually killed close under his horse's nose, when the attempt to halloo "Whoop" convinced him that his ribs were fractured. This mishap gave him a month of idle time, which he has endeavoured to turn to account by assisting in the preparation of this book; and now that he is again in the saddle, he is quite ready to agree that it is an ill wind that blows no good.

THE END.